THE
WARSHIP
Figureheads
OF PORTSMOUTH

THE WARSHIP Figureheads OF PORTSMOUTH

David Pulvertaft

Illustrated by Kevin Dean

In association with the
National Museum of the Royal Navy

The History Press

First published 2009

The History Press
The Mill, Brimscombe Port
Stroud, Gloucestershire, GL5 2QG
www.thehistorypress.co.uk

British Library Cataloguing in Publication Data.
A catalogue record for this book is available from the British
Library.

ISBN 978 0 7524 5076 6

Typesetting and origination by The History Press
Printed in Great Britain

Contents

Foreword

BUCKINGHAM PALACE

Literally thousands of ships were in commission in the Royal Navy from the sixteenth to the nineteenth century. With a few notable exceptions, all of them are long gone. What remains from some, however, are their figureheads: bold HMS *Centurion*, stately HMS *Princess Alice*, restless HMS *Wanderer*, mythical HMS *Unicorn* and many others.

These vivid and colourful reminders of a proud past have remained relatively unstudied and some are threatened with destruction. Rear Admiral David Pulvertaft has recognised the threat and systematically catalogued and identified all the surviving naval figureheads. The first fruits of his labours are presented here in a splendid compendium of the figureheads which survive in Portsmouth, the majority at the National Museum of the Royal Navy.

This book acts as a record of some of those already preserved for posterity. I hope that it will also act as a spur to us all to preserve the rest of this magnificent and spirited part of the Naval Heritage.

Anne

Acknowledgements

I have for many years believed that the figurehead collection of the National Museum of the Royal Navy deserves a book that would do it justice, and have said so whenever given the chance! My first thanks, therefore, go to the directors of the museum who have encouraged me to develop the theme; first Dr Campbell McMurray and then the late Dr Colin White, in whose memory I dedicate this book.

My next thanks go to Kevin Dean who has illustrated this book with his stylish watercolours, as without them it might never have caught a publisher's eye. We both offer our thanks to the staff of the museum who have been most helpful; Matthew Sheldon, Richard Noyce, Stephen Courtney and the gallery attendants who have ensured that Kevin was comfortable during his many hours of work on site.

My research into figureheads has brought me into contact with other historians and restorers in the field, and my thanks go to them for their support and the generous help that they have given me. These include Richard Blundell of Tasmania, John Smith of Fareham, and, in particular, Richard Hunter of Sheffield.

I am also most grateful for the help I have received from Jenny Wraight of the Naval Historical Branch, from Douglas McCarthy of the National Maritime Museum Picture Library and from two vice-presidents of The Society for Nautical Research who agreed to read my draft and offered much valued advice; Dr Alan McGowan and Lieutenant Commander Lawrence Phillips RNR. Despite all this help, any errors that appear in the text are entirely mine.

At The History Press, my thanks go to Amy Rigg who, as Commissioning Editor, saw the potential in the book and ran with it.

Finally, I thank my wife, Mary Rose, for the encouragement she has given me over the many years of research that lie behind this book.

David Pulvertaft
Ottery St Mary

Introduction

The figurehead collection in and around the National Museum of the Royal Navy at Portsmouth is the largest accumulation of British warship figureheads on display in this country, and therefore in the world! The purpose of this book is to describe each of the figureheads in the collection and to provide a short history of the ship in which each one served, giving a flavour of the actions they saw and the places they visited. No attempt is made to analyse the results of the actions nor to assess those who commanded the ships as this is the figureheads' story; one that tells how the ship's name was interpreted by the figurehead carver and its life-history from its creation to the present day. To allow a comparison to be made between the ships, the length and tonnage of each is given and, where Battle Honours have been granted to the ship, these are quoted.

This book is not intended as a guide for visitors to follow round the galleries but rather as a journey through the nineteenth century so that the development of these colourful objects can be appreciated. The watercolour illustrations have been created by Kevin Dean, an artist and designer who now lives near the National Museum of the Royal Navy and who has had an interest in the form and style of these carvings for some years. His work brings to this book something of the artistry that the original carvers provided to the ships themselves. These watercolours and the text are supplemented, where available, by copies of the carvers' original designs and portraits of the individual ships.

For completeness' sake, three appendices have been added; the first describes figureheads that were formerly in the collection but are not there today, the second describes other carvings that are in the collection but are not strictly figureheads, while the third describes other figureheads that are elsewhere in the Portsmouth area.

The Development of the Figurehead

Figureheads were carved for the bows of British fighting ships from early in the sixteenth century until the beginning of the twentieth century in a spectacular range of subjects, sizes and styles, thus formalising the ancient tradition that seafarers had adopted in even earlier times. It was the custom in some countries to paint eyes on the bows of their vessels so that they might better see where they were going, while those with warlike intentions had aggressive animals carved on their bows. Examples from the waters round these islands include the serpents on the prows Viking longboats – still to be seen in the British Museum – and lion and dragon figureheads on the Norman invasion fleet of 1066 – woven into the Bayeux Tapestry.

As fighting ships developed over the centuries, so the shape and size of the bow changed and with it the style of the figurehead. The first examples of figureheads representing the actual name of the British warship on which they were mounted appear in the *Anthony Roll*, a manuscript containing stylised drawings of King Henry VIII's fleet, created in 1546 and presented to the King by Anthony Anthony. Most of the illustrations have a simple horizontal protruding beakhead but those of the

The Unicorne. (British Library Add MS 22047)

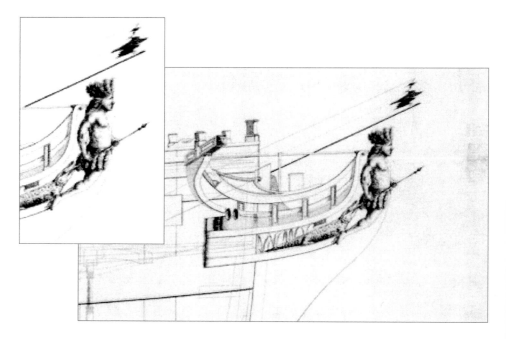

HMS *Crocodile* (1781). (National Maritime Museum – Ship Plan ZAZ 3672)

Unicorn and *Salamander* are surmounted with appropriate animal carvings.

Also included in the *Anthony Roll* is a painting and description of the *Mary Rose*, built in Portsmouth in 1509 but notorious because she capsized off the Isle of Wight in 1545 when preparing to fight off a French invasion. The *Mary Rose* painting does not have any identification on her beakhead but high on her forecastle she is distinguished by a carved rose. Her wreck lay in the silt until a large part of her hull was raised for preservation in 1982. The rose that identified the ship was not discovered until the 2005 diving season and, although not exactly a figurehead, fulfils the same function and is now on display in the Mary Rose Museum.

Warships of the seventeenth century generally displayed carved lions that snarled silently at the enemy but there were no special features that related them to the particular ship. By the eighteenth century, the largest ships were embellished with allegorical carvings of figures and animals with subtleties of meaning that the average sailor would have found hard to understand, while smaller ships were provided with single figures straddling the stem-post. Typical of this style is that from the ship plan of the Portsmouth-built ship HMS *Crocodile*, twenty-four guns, in the form of a native African with feathered headdress and kilt with a crocodile in the trailboards.

Most of the figureheads in the Portsmouth collection are from the nineteenth century by which period each was usually in the form of a single figure that represented in some way the name of the ship. The carvings ranged from full figures – carved from head to toe and standing almost upright – through demi-figures – from the waist up and often holding an object symbolic of the ship's name – to busts – being the torso of the subject with his or her arms cut off above the elbow. Of these three types, the bust was attractive to the authorities on two counts; firstly there were fewer projections to be snagged by the ropes that abounded in sailing ships and, just as importantly, they were less expensive to produce! Not all figureheads were of human form and, where appropriate, all sorts of mammals, birds and even reptiles were carefully carved. The two Portsmouth figureheads still to be seen on the bows of their ships provide a useful illustration of the difference in form between a wooden ship of the line, HMS *Victory* (1765), and an 'ironclad', HMS *Warrior* (1860). Although the figurehead of HMS *Victory* is not her original one, it is almost vertical – surmounting as it does her stem – while that of HMS *Warrior* leans forward with the rake of the bow fitting neatly under the ship's bowsprit.

Ship Names and the Task of the Figurehead Carver

The Admiralty decided what name a particular warship would be given, and this was influenced by the size of the ship and what part it was to play in the nation's affairs. The largest ships of the line were given prestigious names – Portsmouth-built examples being HMS *Britannia* (1762) and HMS *Neptune* (1832). Frigates and smaller vessels were given a wide variety of names such as three of the Portsmouth-built ships of 1842, HMS *Albatros*, HMS *Frolic* and HMS *Firebrand* – being more appropriate to the role that each was to perform. The officers and men who lived, worked, fought and sometimes died in their ships had a very special relationship with them and, of the many features that made up the ship as a whole, the figurehead was the most personal. There are many stories that tell how the figurehead was seen as the personification of the ship and it is not surprising that, when a ship was broken up, the figurehead was not burnt with the material that could not be recycled but was retained as a memento of the ship's life and service.

The art of a successful figurehead carver was to portray the ship's name in an identifiable form. Figureheads carved for ships that were named after members of the royal family or famous generals and admirals were easy to design. Those named after characters from Greek and Roman mythology required some ingenuity and several of these are represented in the Portsmouth collection. Other names were less easy and the carver would then resort to a standard figurehead with an allusion to the name carved in the trailboards. While these additions were often lost when the figurehead was cut from the ship's structure, we are fortunate that the figurehead designs were individually approved by the Admiralty and many of the original carvers' drawings were retained in the Admiralty files. These are now to be found at The National Archives at Kew and, where they exist for the Portsmouth figureheads, are included in this book.

When a ship was being built in one of the dockyards where there was a resident carver, he would prepare a design and estimate of cost that would be sent to the Surveyor of the Navy for approval. For ships building in other yards, such as Pembroke Dockyard in South Wales, the yard would forward a scale drawing of the ship's bow structure including a dotted line within which the figurehead was required to fit.

The Surveyor's office of the Navy Board would send the outline to an independent carver or to one of the yards with a resident carver, asking for a design and estimate. On some occasions copies would be sent to several carvers to create competition between them and

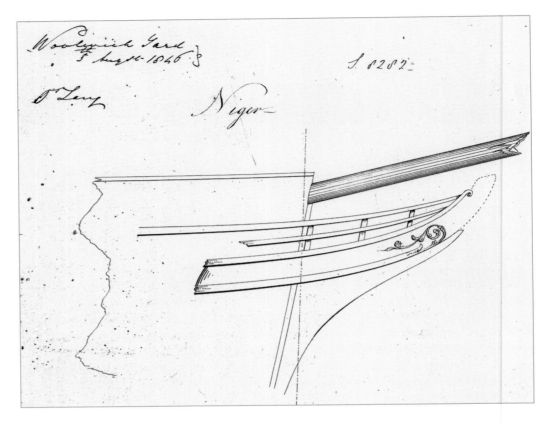

Woolwich Yard drawing of bow structure dated August 1846. (TNA ADM 87/16)

quite often the price quoted in the estimate would not be allowed and a lower figure would be inserted.

The most prolific naval carvers of the period were members of two families; the Hellyers who worked both in Portsmouth and on the Thames at Rotherhithe and the Dickersons who worked in Devonport. As will be found in the individual figurehead descriptions, members of each family carved figureheads that are now in the Portsmouth collection. The dockyard generally provided the carvers with blocks of pitch pine from which the figure was carved, the price paid being dependent on the size and complexity of the work. In addition to the figureheads for ships being built, the resident carvers also created replacements for those found to be decayed and repaired others damaged in action or collisions.

When a warship was no longer required for service, she was either taken to pieces in a royal dockyard, so that certain timbers could be reused, or was sold to a ship-breaking company. And thus it was that the dockyards began to accumulate these relics; the larger ones being mounted in prominent positions round the yards, while the smaller ones were gathered in roomy buildings such as sail lofts or parade sheds.

The Portsmouth Collection

At the beginning of the twentieth century there was a concerted effort to catalogue the figurehead holdings in the royal dockyards. Chatham Dockyard printed its first 'Catalogue of Figureheads, Models, Etc.' in about 1904, while between 1906 and 1911 the Secretary to the Admiral Superintendent at Portsmouth, Mr Mark Edwin Prescott-Frost, created the Portsmouth Dockyard Museum and had its first catalogue printed in 1911. Also in 1911 the Admiralty published its first consolidated 'Admiralty Catalogue of Pictures, Presentation Plate, Figureheads, Models, Relics and Trophies at the Admiralty; on board HM Ships; and in the Naval Establishments at Home and Abroad.' It described over 160 figureheads, the majority of which were in the dockyards of Chatham, Devonport, Portsmouth and Sheerness; twenty-four of them being in Portsmouth Dockyard. More details are given on page 36.

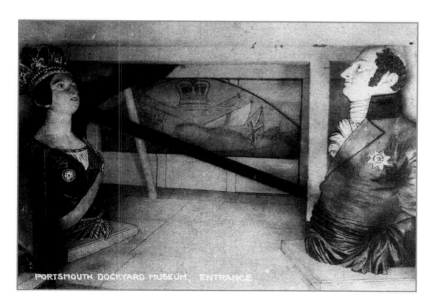

The entrance to the Dockyard Museum. (Richard Hunter Archive)

The Portsmouth Dockyard Museum had at its entrance two very large royal bust figureheads from the Portsmouth-built ships HMS *Royal Sovereign* and HMS *Royal Frederick*, each measuring more than 8ft in height. More details of these can be found in Appendix I.

Inside the Dockyard Museum. (Richard Hunter Archive)

In 1913 and 1914 a series of articles were written on the dockyard collections by the Honorary Secretary of the Society for Nautical Research, Mr Douglas Owen, in the Society's journal, *The Mariner's Mirror*. He had realised that, for one reason or another, many figureheads had by then been lost and hoped that, by describing the most significant of those that remained, he would create an interest in them and provide a foundation on which others might build. He urged that the collections should be assembled in 'a great Naval Museum' and asked why Mr Frost's achievement at Portsmouth could not be followed in Devonport where the largest collection had accumulated in a variety of available spaces. Mr Frost's upstairs gallery he described as 'a delightful little museum where all are displayed with the most loving care'.

When the National Maritime Museum was established in 1937, the Admiralty gave nineteen figureheads from the Devonport collection but Mr Frost's museum was not affected. When the dockyards at Sheerness and Chatham were closed in 1960 and 1984 respectively, there was a considerable dispersion of their figureheads, largely to naval shore-establishments and it is some of these that have made up the later additions to the original Portsmouth collection.

In the years since the National Museum of the Royal Navy was created in 1971, the galleries have been developed in such a way that most of the figureheads are on the first floor of the Victory Gallery with others in convenient spaces both inside and outside the museum itself.

The Figureheads

HMS *Victory*	HMS *Cleopatra*
HMS *Warrior*	HMS *Trafalgar*
HMS *Bellerophon*	HMS *Eurydice*
HMS *Illustrious*	*Black Eagle*, formerly HMS *Firebrand*
HMS *Apollo*	*Princess Alice*
HMS *Calliope*	HMS *Grampus*, formerly HMS *Tremendous*
HMS *Benbow*	*Fairy*
HMS *Glasgow*	HMS *Calypso*
HMS *Minerva*	HMS *Caradoc*
HMS *Madagascar*	*Elfin*
HMS *Carnatic*	*Unknown Lady*
HMS *Bellerophon*, formerly HMS *Waterloo*	HMS *Cruizer*
HMS *Orestes*	HMS *Malacca*
HMS *Asia*	HMS *Wanderer*
HMS *Rolla*	HMS *Peterel*
HMS *Actaeon*	HMS *Warrior*
Royal Adelaide	HMS *Centurion*
HMS *Blazer*	HMS *Espiegle*

HMS *Victory* – 1765

1st Rate, 100 guns, 2,142bm, 186ft
Battle Honours: Ushant 1781, St Vincent 1797, Trafalgar 1805

The Ship – pre-1800

The keel of HMS *Victory* was laid down in one of Chatham Dockyard's dry docks in July 1759, but it was not until May 1765 that she was floated off; a classic 100-gun ship of the line. She lay in Ordinary at Chatham until 1778 when she was fitted for sea and first commissioned in March that year.

The next few years saw her leading the Channel Fleet in two encounters with the French off Ushant – each resulting from France's involvement in the American War of Independence. The first was as Admiral Keppel's flagship in July 1778 but, though damaging broadsides were exchanged, the outcome was inconclusive and no Battle Honours were awarded. The second, in December 1781, was as Admiral Kempenfelt's flagship when, despite being numerically inferior to the French escorting fleet, he managed to cut out fifteen merchantmen from the convoy bound from Brest to the West Indies.

In the next few years *Victory* flew the flag of several other admirals but in 1795 she became the flagship of Admiral Sir John Jervis's Mediterranean Fleet, blockading Toulon for most of 1796 and attacking the Spanish fleet off the Portuguese coast in the Battle of St Vincent in February 1797. The decisive victory prevented the Spanish fleet joining up with the French at Brest and regained the initiative for Britain in the naval war. Admiral Jervis was made Earl St Vincent, while Commodore Nelson – who had commanded HMS *Captain* with distinction – was made a Knight of the Bath.

Victory returned home and, after a short period as a hospital ship for prisoners of war, entered Chatham Dockyard in 1800 for what turned out to be a lengthy repair.

The Figurehead – pre-1800

Victory's first figurehead was a massive accumulation of figures that was thought appropriate for a 1st Rate of the eighteenth century. Measuring some 24ft high and 18ft wide, the carvers were Richard Crichley and William Savage. Their carvers' model has survived and is now in the National Maritime Museum at Greenwich and has been used for the illustration opposite. Happily, the specification has also survived so we can identify the individual components. The whole thing is surmounted by a bust of King George III, his head adorned with laurels and his body and shoulders worked in rich armour. Under him is a shield surrounded by four cherubs' heads and wings representing the four winds and blowing out success over the four quarters of the globe. The principle figure on the starboard side is Britannia, seated on a triumphal arch supporting the King's bust with one hand and one foot trampling down envy, discord and faction. Above Britannia is a flying figure representing Peace, crowning Britannia with laurels and holding a branch of palms. Behind the arch is the British lion trampling on trophies of war while under it are figures representing Europe and America. Finally at the rear is a cherub holding a cornucopia representing the consequences of victory and a branch of palms as an emblem of peace.

On the port side, the equivalent figures are Victory trampling down rebellion with the flying figure of Fame above her, trumpet in one hand sounding a victory call while holding a branch of palms in the other. A shield with the royal escutcheon and the imperial crown replaces the lion while the figures supporting the arch represent Asia and Africa. Finally, the cherub holding a pair of compasses in one hand and pointing to a globe with the other is indicating the mathematics of navigation and success in all parts of the world.

For their work, the carvers were allowed £180 for the figurehead, £15 for a clay model and £7.11.0 for some elaborate trailboards.

The Ship – post-1800

With war looming, *Victory* was made ready and, in May 1803, she became Vice Admiral Lord Nelson's flagship and sailed for the Mediterranean. A long blockade of Toulon, a chase to the West Indies and the scene was set for one of the last sea battles of the sailing navy – the Battle of Trafalgar in October 1805. The combined Franco-Spanish fleet under Vice Admiral Comte de Villeneuve broke out from Cadiz on the Atlantic coast of Spain and the two great fleets entered battle. Nelson's tactics were unconventional, the seamanship and gunnery of the Royal Navy were far superior to that of the enemy and a resounding victory resulted. When the fighting was at its fiercest, Nelson was shot by a French marksman. He was taken below but died that afternoon.

Badly damaged, *Victory* was towed to Gibraltar and later returned home carrying the body of her dead admiral. After extensive repairs she served in the Baltic and off the coasts of Spain until 1812 when she returned to Portsmouth, marking the end of her sea-going life and the start of another period of repairs and modernisation. In 1824 she became the flagship for the Port Admiral, she was saved from the 'disposal list' in 1831 and in 1889 became the flagship for the Commander-in-Chief; a position that she holds to this day.

By 1920 her condition had deteriorated such that she was in danger of sinking at her moorings. The Society for Nautical Research led a national appeal to 'Save the *Victory*' and in 1922 she was docked in No.2 Dock where she remains today – restored to her 1805 appearance.

John Player & Sons cigarette card, 1912.

The Figurehead – post-1800

During *Victory*'s lengthy repairs of 1800–03 at Chatham, the original figurehead was removed and a replacement was carved. Chatham Yard actually forwarded three alternative figurehead designs in March 1802 and of these, 'No.2' was approved at a cost of £50 but unfortunately, while the letters of approval have survived in The National Archives, the designs are not filed with them. In June 1815 during her modernisation at Portsmouth, Edward Hellyer, the resident carver there, submitted a design for another figurehead with an estimate for £65 which was accepted by the Surveyor of the Navy. As the Chatham figurehead was by then only thirteen years old, a replacement was probably needed because the shape of *Victory*'s bow was significantly altered during that period. Again, no designs were retained with the authorisation papers.

The question of exactly what figurehead *Victory* had at the Battle of Trafalgar has been widely debated over the years. There has been much speculation that it was in the form of the Royal Arms surmounted by a crown but with a sailor and a Royal Marine as the supporters. A drawing of this arrangement was included in a set of twenty-five 'Ships' Figureheads' cigarette cards issued by John Player & Sons in 1912, claiming that this was believed to be the one carried at the battle. This view is given some credence by the fact that almost all the other cards in the set were of figureheads that were then surviving so that the artist had access to them. Was there, perhaps, evidence available to him that has since been lost?

Present wisdom is that *Victory*'s figurehead at the Battle of Trafalgar was that which is now on her bow and is shown opposite. The present carving is a replacement, carved at Portsmouth in the dockyard workshops in the late 1980s.

HMS *Warrior* – 1781-1857

3rd Rate, 74 guns, 1,642bm, 169ft
Battle Honours: The Saints 1782, Copenhagen 1801

The Ship

Built in Portsmouth Dockyard and launched there in October 1781, she was the first ship to bear the name, but see also HMS *Warrior* of 1860 on page 90. She saw action in the West Indies against the French fleet in April 1782 with Admiral Sir George Rodney at the Battle of The Saints, restoring British supremacy in the area. In 1801 she was part of Admiral Sir Hyde Parker's Baltic fleet when he attacked the Danish fleet in the strongly defended harbour of Copenhagen. While *Warrior* was not one of the ships that went close inshore with Vice Admiral Nelson, all the ships involved in the battle were subsequently granted the Battle Honour. In 1805 she was one of the squadron, under Admiral Sir Robert Calder, blockading the north-west tip of Spain and intended to intercept a Franco-Spanish fleet returning from the West Indies. The two fleets did engage but 'Calder's Action' was indecisive and no Battle Honours were awarded.

In the peace that followed Trafalgar, *Warrior* crossed the Atlantic on at least two occasions, escorting convoys to the West Indies, but by 1818 her sea-going service came to an end and she became the receiving ship at Chatham and then

Detail of contemporary ship model.
(Science & Society Picture Library)

Woolwich. In 1840 her status was again reduced and she became a convict hulk. She was taken to pieces at Woolwich in December 1857.

The Figurehead

All that remains of *Warrior*'s figurehead is the warrior's head and neck but the ship plan in the collection of the National Maritime Museum and a contemporary model of the ship now in the Science Museum, London each show a carving that is typical of the late eighteenth century. Figureheads of that period were of full length, straddling the ship's bow, and it was not until some years later that the Navy Board cut costs by limiting them to simple busts.

The carving has been at Portsmouth for many years as it was listed as being there in the 1911 Admiralty Catalogue and in the first edition of the Portsmouth Dockyard Museum catalogue of the same date. In all probability, when the ship was broken up, the body of the figurehead was found to be rotten and only the head was saved.

HMS *Bellerophon* – 1789-1836

3rd Rate, 74 guns, 1634bm, 168ft
Battle Honours: Glorious First of June 1794, Cornwallis' Retreat 1795, Nile 1798, Trafalgar 1805

The Ship

Built on the River Medway at Frindsbury, she was the first ship to bear the name *Bellerophon* and was known affectionately in the navy as 'Billy Ruff'n'. She saw more action than any other ship represented in the Portsmouth collection, starting in 1794 when she was the first ship to engage the French fleet at the Battle of the Glorious First of June under Admiral Lord Howe. In 1795 she was part of the fleet that achieved a masterly retreat under Vice Admiral Cornwallis from a greatly superior French fleet. In 1798 she took part in the Battle of the Nile at Aboukir Bay, the fleet being under the then Rear Admiral Horatio Nelson, and in 1805 she distinguished herself at the Battle of Trafalgar under Vice Admiral Lord Nelson.

It was on her quarterdeck that Napoleon Bonaparte surrendered after the Battle of Waterloo in 1815. He was brought back to England in her before being taken to exile in St Helena. From 1816 to 1836 she was a convict hulk at Sheerness (renamed *Captivity* in 1824) and was sold for breaking up in 1836.

The Figurehead

In the Golden Age of Mythology, Bellerophon was a gallant young warrior who was persuaded to fight the Chimaera; a fearful monster; part lion, part goat and part dragon. He used Minerva's magic to catch the winged horse, Pegasus, and with its help slew the monster.

In Edward Fraser's biography of the ship, he describes her figurehead as the figure of Bellerophon, naked except for a short red cloak flung back on his shoulders, riding bareback on Pegasus – its wings spread wide. Bellerophon had his right arm raised and ready to strike with his javelin.

When the ship was broken up in 1836, the Admiral Superintendent at Portsmouth happened to be Sir Frederick Maitland who had commanded *Bellerophon* when Napoleon surrendered in 1815. He bought the figurehead and some of her stern carvings and had them installed in the mould-loft of the dockyard but most of the carving must by then have decayed as it was only Bellerophon's helmeted head that was saved.

FIGUREHEAD COLOURS

Although the figureheads in the Portsmouth collection are all colourfully painted, most of them would have been painted white during their service at sea. There were of course exceptions and some commanding officers were known to have paid for parts of their figureheads to be gilded. However, the evidence from contemporary paintings and early photographs indicates that the majority of warship figureheads were painted white; a conclusion that is supported by an unusual request to the Navy Board in 1814 that the figurehead that had been approved for HMS *Nelson* should be 'properly painted in colours'.

HMS *Illustrious* – 1803-1868

3rd Rate, 74 guns
Battle Honours: Basque Roads 1809, Java 1811

The Ship

Built by Randall of Rotherhithe on the Thames, HMS *Illustrious* was launched in September 1803. In 1809 she was one of Admiral Lord Gambier's Channel Fleet that blockaded the French fleet anchored off Rochefort in the Basque Roads. Determined to rid the Bay of Biscay of the continuing French threat, the Admiralty despatched fire ships that were manoeuvred into the anchorage causing much confusion and most of the French fleet to run aground. The action was, however, not as successful as had been hoped and resulted in much subsequent acrimony between the senior officers involved.

In 1809 *Illustrious* was amongst the fleet that supported an expedition of 40,000 troops tasked with capturing the Island of Walcheren in Holland and destroying the local dockyards, thus preventing their use by the French fleet. The next year saw her off Mauritius where a force of 10,000 troops were landed before the French surrendered the island as well as eight men-of-war lying in Port Louis. In 1811 she was part of an attack on the Island of Java, then in the possession of the Dutch. Eight thousand men were landed – including a naval brigade – and, while Batavia surrendered quite quickly, there were fierce exchanges before the island was taken.

From 1848 she undertook harbour duties as a guard-ship, a hospital ship, the Portsmouth gunnery training ship and finally the cadet training ship and thus the predecessor of HMS *Britannia* at Dartmouth. She was taken to pieces at Portsmouth in 1868.

The Figurehead

The first figurehead design included in the Admiralty records was submitted by Edward Hellyer of Portsmouth in June 1808 showing George III wearing a breast-plate and a crown. He asked for £24 to carve the bust but was allowed only £21.

Perhaps that figurehead was damaged in the 1811 action, as in June 1816 Hellyer submitted another design showing the King in an ermine cape with the insignia of the Order of the Garter and an estimate of £21.

This appears to have been rejected in favour of a coat of arms for which he was allowed only £16 for the work. The records do not show when the surviving figurehead was carved but, as it is a bust of George III, it must have been before 1820.

Left: Design by Edward Hellyer dated 1808. (TNA – ADM 106/1885)

Below: Design by Edward Hellyer dated 1816. (TNA – ADM 106/1888)

HMS *Apollo* – 1805-1856

5th Rate, 38 guns, 1,086bm, 154ft
Battle Honours: China 1842, Crimea 1854

The Ship

Named after one of the greatest gods of both Greek and Roman mythology, and the fifth ship to bear the name, she was built by Parsons at Bursledon and launched there in 1805. She saw active service in the Mediterranean – including a number of skirmishes with the French between 1807 and 1814. In 1822 there were plans to convert her into a royal yacht and Edward Hellyer of Portsmouth submitted a figurehead design that incorporated a bust, royal arms and trophies – all for £40 – but the conversion was never completed. By 1838 she had become something rather less glamorous – a troopship – and it was in this role that she took part in the Yang-Tse-Kiang expedition that ended the First Opium War with China, 1840–42.

Shortly before the end of her service she was converted into a store ship and this was her task when she took part in the expedition to the Crimea. She was broken up in 1856.

The Figurehead

Apollo was the son of Jupiter and was the mythological embodiment of the sun. He was renowned for destroying the serpent Python with arrows and was generally represented holding a bow or sometimes a lyre.

The surviving figurehead is not the original 1805 carving as a new one was carved by Edward Hellyer of Portsmouth in 1817.

Design by Edward Hellyer & Son dated 1817. (TNA – ADM 106/1889)

No explanation is given why a new figurehead was required but he submitted two designs; the standing figure for £15 – shown here – and a bust for £6. A carver's note explained that the standing figure would have had an arrow in his right hand and a bow in his left but the Surveyor of the Navy chose the less expensive bust and allowed £6 for the work, the figurehead that is on display today.

Unfortunately, when the figurehead was cut from the ship, the trailboard carvings were left behind but they would, almost certainly, have included the bow and arrow that could not be incorporated into a bust figurehead.

HMS *Calliope* – 1808-1826

Brig-sloop, 10 guns, 237bm, 90ft

The Ship

When the first catalogue of the Portsmouth Dockyard Museum was published in 1911, there was some doubt about the origin of this figurehead; the entry saying: 'Believed to be that of *Calliope*, brig sloop, ten guns, built on the Thames and launched in 1808.'

Assuming the curator of the day was right in his belief, she was built by John Dudman at Deptford and launched there in July 1808. Being a small vessel, she was not involved in any major actions but in October 1810 she did capture the privateer *La Contesse d'Hambourg* – fourteen guns – in the North Sea.

She was based in Portsmouth from 1817 and became the tender to the royal yacht, *Royal George*, in 1825. She was taken to pieces at Portsmouth in 1829.

The Figurehead

In Greek mythology, Calliope was one of the nine muses, daughters of Zeus, she being the Muse of Epic Poetry. The muses were represented as handsome and modest virgins, dressed in long tunics; Calliope's identifying feature being either a tablet and stylus or a roll of parchment. From the nature of the carving and the fact that HMS *Calliope* was taken to pieces in Portsmouth, one can see why she was thought to have come from that ship, even though the direct evidence may have been lost in the eighty or so years between her being broken up and the Dockyard Museum catalogue being first published.

Two other *Calliope* figureheads have survived the passage of time; that from the 1837–83 6th Rate is in the Devonport collection while the bow decoration from the 1884–1951 screw corvette is preserved in the headquarters of the Royal Naval Reserve at Gateshead. It was the 1884 *Calliope* that distinguished herself by steaming out of Apia Bay, Samoa, into the teeth of a hurricane that wrecked six German and American warships.

TAILBOARD CARVINGS

The bow structure that carried the figurehead created a panel – known as the 'trailboard' – that allowed the carver to continue his work downwards and backwards from the figurehead itself in *trailboard carvings*. Ships named after military men were given implements of war such as cannons, banners and swords; those named after rivers would have a suggestion of flowing water while those named after mythological characters might depict some part of the story – see the design for HMS *Eurydice* on page 64.

More often than not, when the figurehead was removed from the ship, the trailboard carvings were lost, making the surviving carvers' designs particularly informative.

HMS *Benbow* – 1813-1895

3rd Rate, 72 guns, 1,773bm, 176ft
Battle Honour: Syria 1840

The Ship

Built at the private yard of John Brent of Rotherhithe and launched there in February 1813, she was a 3rd Rate of seventy-two guns and the first of three ships of the Royal Navy to be named after Vice Admiral John Benbow, Commander-in-Chief of the West Indies during the War of the Spanish Succession, who died of wounds sustained in a battle with a French squadron in 1702.

In 1840 HMS *Benbow* saw action blockading the Syrian coast as part of the Anglo-Austrian-Turkish fleet preventing the Egyptians, who had occupied Syria, making further advances against Turkey. In the same campaign she took part in an attack on Torosa and the bombardment of St Jean D'Acre.

In 1848 she became a marine barrack ship, in 1854 an accommodation ship for Russian prisoners of war and in 1859 a coal hulk at Sheerness. She was sold to Castles of Woolwich for breaking up in 1895.

The Figurehead

Carved in the form of a bust of Vice Admiral John Benbow, he is shown wearing armour that has been painted black (as he is seen today) and metallic silver in the 1950s. He has a cravat and wig of the period.

Once ashore, the figurehead became part of the Chatham collection where he was included in the 1911 Admiralty Catalogue, remaining there until the 1940s when he was transferred to Portsmouth. Today he is the first figurehead of the collection that a visitor will see, greeting new arrivals as they walk from the Victory Gate of the Naval Base towards HMS *Victory*, the National Museum of the Royal Navy and the many other attractions.

THE 1911 ADMIRALTY CATALOGUE

Early in the twentieth century the Lord Commissioners of the Admiralty decided that a permanent record should be made of all plate and property of historic value or interest within the service. The result was their 'Catalogue of Pictures, Presentation Plate, Figureheads, Models, Relics and Trophies at the Admiralty; on board H.M. Ships; and in the Naval Establishments at Home or Abroad' dated 30 April 1911.

As far as figureheads were concerned, the catalogue could not be comprehensive as it did not include those still fitted to ships in commission nor those on ships that had been converted for a support role such as accommodation, store, training or prison ships. Despite this limitation, the catalogue includes over 150 figureheads and, though not illustrated, lists – by location – the name of the ship from which it came and the size and form of the carving. The principal figurehead collections that can be found in this catalogue are at Chatham (fifty named items and others not identified), Sheerness (four), Portsmouth (fourteen) and Devonport (sixty-five) and Pembroke (five). The catalogue thus provides an excellent baseline from which changes can be recorded, whether they be additions, losses or movements

HMS *Glasgow* – 1814-1828

4th Rate, 50 guns, 1,260bm, 159ft
Battle Honours: Algiers 1816, Navarino 1827

The Ship

Built in the private yard of Wigram & Green of Blackwall, she was one of a class of frigates known as 'fir built' as they were constructed from pitch pine.

At the end of the Napoleonic War, the British Government resolved to deal with piracy and the slave trade along the North African coastline. Admiral Lord Exmouth offered treaties with the Deys (governors) of Tunis, Tripoli and Algiers but the Dey of Algiers rejected the offer and so, in August 1816, suffered a bombardment by a combined Anglo-Dutch fleet. The Moors responded and HMS *Glasgow* sustained ten killed and thirty-seven wounded; but the fleet's firepower was huge, *Glasgow's* contribution to the bombardment being over 3,000 rounds. Over 1,000 Christian slaves were released. See also *Queen Charlotte* on page 106.

She also fought in the Battle of Navarino in 1827 when Vice Admiral Sir Edward Codrington commanded a British, French and Russian fleet against a Turko-Egyptian fleet. His flagship was HMS *Asia* and a brief description of the action will be found under that ship on page 50.

HMS *Glasgow* was taken to pieces in Chatham Dockyard in 1829.

The Figurehead

It is unusual for a frigate to have a full-length figure as her figurehead – explained, perhaps, by the carver's wish to show a kilted soldier to represent the city of Glasgow.

When the ship was taken to pieces in 1829, the figurehead was taken into the Chatham collection and was recorded as being there in the musters of 1911 and 1938. By 1949 he had been transferred to the collection at HMS *Ganges*, the boys' training establishment at Shotley, Suffolk, where he remained until its closure in 1976. The figurehead then stood outside the Royal Naval Hospital, Haslar, for some years before being transferred to the National Museum of the Royal Navy in 1983.

From *Sailing Ships of War 1800-1860* by
Sir Alan Moore.

HMS *Minerva* – 1820-1895

5th Rate, 46 guns, 1,082bm, 152ft

The Ship

Built in Portsmouth Dockyard and launched there in June 1820, she was the sixth ship to bear the name – a frigate of the Modified Leda Class. The Greek and Roman gods proved to be popular names for minor warships of the nineteenth century and Minerva, daughter of Jupiter and the Roman goddess of the arts, crafts and war, was one of these.

HMS *Minerva* had an uneventful career and by 1848 was in Ordinary at Portsmouth with her masts and rigging removed. From 1870 she was used as a workshop for artificers of the Steam Reserve until she was finally sold in 1895 to the Bevis Engineering & Shipbreaking Co. for breaking up.

The Figurehead

With the ship building in Portsmouth Dockyard, the resident carvers, Edward Hellyer & Son, submitted their design in March 1819 with an estimate for £15 and £3.8.0 for each trailboard. A note beside the drawing records that the left hand was to be holding a shield.

Design by Edward Hellyer & Son dated 1819. (TNA – ADM 106/1889)

The design was typical of the representation of Minerva as her birth was said not to be a normal one but she sprang full-armed from her father's brain! She was therefore usually depicted as wearing a coat of mail and a helmet and carrying a spear. The Surveyor of the Navy did not approve the design – a full-length figure being exceptional for such a small ship – his reply instructed 'Direct the Officers to cause in this instance a bust of Minerva to be carved and allow the carvers £8 for the same, but we do not approve of having carved work in the trailboards.'

The bust figurehead shows Minerva wearing her armour and helmet but without reference to her spear or shield. When the ship was broken up, the figurehead was kept by the Bevis family for several generations but by 1967 she was in a very poor condition and the owner gave her to the dockyard for restoration and display. She was repaired by the dockyard shipwrights and, as was then the practice, she was covered in a thin coat of fibreglass, the intention being to place her outside the Central Office Block. Happily, she was soon put into the much more suitable climate of the Victory Gallery.

HMS *Madagascar* – 1822-1863

5th Rate, 46 guns, 1,167bm, 159ft

The Ship

Built by the East India Company in Bombay and launched there in November 1822, HMS *Madagascar* was originally ordered in 1819 as one of the Seringapatam Class of frigates but was re-ordered in 1820 in a slightly modified form as one of the Druid Class. Like many other Indian-built ships, she was constructed of teak.

She saw service in the Mediterranean and in the East Indies and in the early 1840s she was one of the ships of the West Africa Squadron as part of the Royal Navy's effort to suppress the slave trade.

In 1846 she became a provision depot at Plymouth; in 1853 she was moved to Rio de Janeiro as a receiving ship and she was finally sold there in 1863.

Design by Edward Hellyer & Son dated 1812.
(TNA – ADM 106/1886)

The Figurehead

Only the figurehead's head and neck have survived but it is most likely that a frigate of this period would have been given a simple bust.

The design shown here was submitted for the earlier ship of the name, captured from the French in 1811 and renamed HMS *Madagascar*. The drawing was forwarded in 1812 by Edward Hellyer, figurehead carver of Portsmouth, with an estimate of £6. Most of the carvers' designs were pen and ink drawings but on this occasion the carver added colour and included a cornucopia of tropical fruits in the trailboards. The 1822 figurehead would probably have been of a similar style.

There is no documentation to explain how the figurehead of a ship that was broken up in Brazil in 1863 was donated to the National Museum of the Royal Navy in 1995. The donor understands that one of his ancestors who lived in Brazil in the 1860s found the figurehead being burned on a bonfire and was only able to save the head! When it returned to the UK is not known but it was restored in 1996 by Allan Mechen of Southampton who confirmed that the figure is carved from teak.

HMS *Carnatic* – 1823-1914

3rd Rate, 72 guns, 1,790bm, 177ft

The Ship

Built in Portsmouth Dockyard, she was the second ship of the name; the first – launched in 1783 – having been paid for by the East India Company and named after the geographical area to the south-east of India, *Karnatic*. Launched in Portsmouth in October 1823, she was a 3rd Rate of seventy-two guns but was never commissioned. She was laid up in Portsmouth and used first as a store, then in 1860 as a coal hulk and finally as a powder store on loan at first to the War Department between 1886 and 1891 and subsequently by the Admiralty. She was sold in 1914 and broken up in Germany.

The Figurehead

When the ship was sold for breaking up, the Admiralty instructed – in a letter of 4 May 1914 – that the figurehead should be allocated to the Museum at Portsmouth. The figurehead did not feature in the 1911 Admiralty Catalogue as he was still on the ship's bow but he was included in the 1919 edition of the Portsmouth Dockyard Museum's catalogue.

A bust in the form of an Indian wearing a beaded and jewelled turban and a chain of office, his tunic was at one time painted in stripes.

HMS *Bellerophon* – 1824-1892

2nd Rate, 80 guns
Battle Honours: Syria 1840, Crimea 1854

Formerly HMS Waterloo *1818-1824*

The Ship

Originally laid down in Portsmouth Dockyard as HMS *Talavera*, she was renamed HMS *Waterloo* before her launch in October 1818 but was immediately placed in Ordinary and was not finally fitted for sea until 1836, having by then been renamed HMS *Bellerophon*, the second ship to have been given the name.

She joined the Mediterranean Fleet in 1836 and, when war broke out between Egypt and Turkey in 1840, was involved in the bombardment of Acre – being granted her Battle Honour 'Syria 1840'. She rejoined the Mediterranean Fleet in 1847 and, after deploying to the Black Sea, took part in the bombardment of Sevastopol – being awarded her second Battle Honour 'Crimea 1854'.

On her return to home waters, she was decommissioned in 1855 and became the receiving ship at Portsmouth in 1856, remaining there until she was eventually sold to be broken up by J. Read of Portsmouth in 1892.

The Figurehead

A contemporary article in the *Hampshire Telegraph* reports that, when HMS *Waterloo* was launched in October 1818, her figurehead was a fine full-length representation of the Duke of Wellington – entirely appropriate to a ship that was being named to honour his glorious victory at Waterloo. Admiralty letter books record that the carving was created by Messrs Hellyer & Co. at Portsmouth.

When the ship was renamed *Bellerophon* in 1824, a figurehead in the form of the Duke would not have been appropriate and a replacement would have been necessary. While the *Bellerophon* of 1786 may have had a complex figurehead of the young warrior mounted on Pegasus, the winged horse, by the 1820s such extravagance was not permitted and a simple bust of a warrior figure was typical of the period. Although no records of the design or its cost have survived, it will almost certainly have also been carved at Portsmouth by the Hellyer family.

From *Sailing Ships of War 1800–1860* by Sir Alan Moore.

HMS *Orestes* — 1824-1905

Sloop, 18 guns, 460bm, 110ft

The Ship

Built in Portsmouth Dockyard and launched there in May 1824, she was the fifth ship to have borne the name. Here is another ship whose name comes from classical mythology, but quite why their Lordships chose Orestes is a mystery. Certainly, he was the son of Agamemnon and became king of Mycenae and Argos, but the several versions of the legends about him all involve murder, revenge, madness and purification; not exactly subjects to inspire the ship's company!

HMS *Orestes* saw service in Halifax in the mid-1820s and was based in Cork in the early 1830s. In 1832 she was one of the squadron of small ships despatched at the outbreak of civil war in Portugal to protect British interests. She spent almost a year on the Douro River, often caught in the cross-fire of the opposing sides but with few casualties. In the 1830s and 1840s she served in the Mediterranean and on the Cape of Good Hope Station before returning to Portsmouth. With the steady transition in the fleet from sail to steam, coal depots were needed and in 1852 she assumed this role and subsequently lost her name and became simply 'C 28' so that the name *Orestes* could be used for an 1860 wood screw corvette. She was sold for commercial use in about 1911.

The Figurehead

The figurehead is a simple helmeted male bust with armour protecting his upper arms over which is draped a classical tunic. No records have been found amongst the Admiralty papers to identify who carved him but, as the ship was built at Portsmouth Dockyard, it will probably have been Edward Hellyer or his son, James, the resident carvers. Nor is it recorded exactly when the figurehead was removed from the hulk and placed in the Portsmouth Dockyard Museum. For some reason he is not listed in the 1911 Admiralty Catalogue but he is included in the first edition of the Portsmouth Museum catalogue of the same date. He was fully restored in the late 1980s.

The design sketch below was that submitted by J.E. & J. Hellyer of Portsmouth in April 1860 for the next HMS *Orestes*, the wood screw corvette mentioned above, then building in Sheerness Dockyard. The design was drawn by the carvers on a scale drawing of the ship's bow provided by Sheerness, fitting neatly within the dotted line and including in the trailboards the classical implements of war.

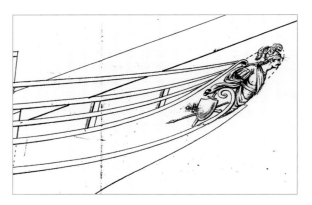

Design by J.E. & J. Hellyer dated 1860.
(TNA – ADM 87/74)

HMS *Asia* – 1824-1908

2nd Rate, 84 guns, 2,289bm, 197ft
Battle Honours: Navarino 1827, Syria 1840

The Ship

The first British vessel with the geographical name *Asia* was a hulk, purchased at Cadiz in 1694. Two 3rd Rate ships followed before this 2nd Rate was built at Bombay and was launched there in January 1824. She was Admiral Sir Edward Codrington's flagship at the Battle of Navarino in 1827 during the Greek War of Independence when the combined British, French and Russian fleet, supporting the Greeks, fought a Turco-Egyptian fleet three times its size that was attempting to restore Turkish control. Sixty enemy ships were burnt or sunk, the remainder being driven ashore. The battle was the last general action fought between wooden sailing ships, *Asia* having nineteen of her crew killed and fifty-seven wounded.

Despite growing obsolescence, she also took part in the blockade of the Syrian coast in 1840 and was used as a transport ship during the Crimean War. In 1858 she became the guardship to the ships in Ordinary at Portsmouth where she remained until she was sold for breaking up in 1908.

The Figurehead

Compared with other bust figureheads of the period, this carving is very compact and does not incorporate the folds of simulated cloth that usually wrap the base of the torso. Photographs of the ship's bow before she was sold for breaking up show the figurehead sitting neatly on scrolls with the drapery round his neck flowing down the trailboards. He is also wearing a white turban so the present colourful one is a modern restorer's addition.

The figureheads of many later ships that were built in Bombay were carved in England and shipped to India but such records do not exist for the period when this figurehead was carved. His unusual style suggests that he might have been carved in Bombay while the ship was building there.

The figurehead was clearly removed from the ship before she was sold in 1908 as he appears in the 1911 Admiralty Catalogue amongst the figureheads in Portsmouth Dockyard, described as 'Figure of a Rajah (bust)'.

From *Sailing Ships of War 1800-1860* by
Sir Alan Moore.

HMS *Rolla* – 1829-1868

Brig-sloop, 10 guns, 231bm, 90ft

The Ship

Built in Plymouth Dockyard and launched there in December 1829, she was one of the many Cherokee Class flush-decked brigs and the second brig to bear the name. For such a small vessel she travelled widely, including the Cape of Good Hope and Africa Station between 1833 and 1837, off the Spanish and African coasts between 1839 and 1842, paying off in Chatham in 1842. She served again off Africa between 1844 and 1846, including a period off the east coast. She returned eventually to Portsmouth in 1847 where for many years she was used variously as a training brig and as a tender to HMS *Victory*.

She was taken to pieces in Portsmouth Dockyard in 1868.

The Figurehead

The reason for selecting the name *Rolla* in 1807 for the first brig of that name is somewhat obscure but it may well have been the popularity of a production by Sheridan of the play *The Spaniards in Peru* or *The Death of Rolla* in which a Peruvian general

National Maritime Museum PAF 6021.

Rolla is the hero. A contemporary illustration of the general shows him in a classical tunic, the belt of which has a buckle very similar to that of the figurehead. Perhaps this was the inspiration for the 1807 carver that would have then been followed by James Dickerson, the resident carver at Plymouth Dockyard, for the 1829 ship. His estimate for £3.0.0 was approved.

When the ship was taken to pieces in 1868, the figurehead would normally have been expected to join the Portsmouth collection but it somehow found its way to the Chatham museum where it was listed in the 1911 Admiralty Catalogue. The Chatham figureheads were moved around the yard over the years and by 1957 *Rolla* could be found outside the Admiral Superintendent's house – he being too small to join the rank of larger figureheads beside the Admiral's Walk. When Chatham Dockyard was closed in 1984, *Rolla* was transferred to HMS *Sussex*, the Sussex Division of the RNR, and there he remained until its closure in 1994 when he came to join the Portsmouth collection in the National Museum of the Royal Navy.

HMS *Actaeon* — 1831-1889

6th Rate, 28 guns, 620bm, 121ft
Battle Honour: China 1856-60

The Ship

Named after a huntsman in Greek mythology, she was the fifth ship named *Actaeon* to serve in the Royal Navy. Built in Portsmouth Dockyard and launched there in January 1831, she saw twenty-five years of service before being converted to a surveying ship and reduced to eighteen guns in 1856. She made many useful surveys for the fleet in the Far East during the Second Opium War with China and, under Admiral Sir Michael Seymour, took part in the naval bombardment of Canton in 1857. While her captain, Captain William Thornton Bate, was mortally wounded, the action allowed British and French troops to take the city. In 1860 she took part in further operations including the capture of the Taku Forts.

By 1866 she had completed her active service and was lent first as a cholera hospital ship to the Guardians of the Poor at Cowes, Isle of Wight, and then in 1870 to the Cork Harbour Board as a hulk. In 1874 she returned to Portsmouth where, with the hulk of HMS *Vernon*, she became part of HMS *Excellent*, established 'to study the new science of torpedo warfare and the application of electrics to gunnery'. She was replaced in 1885 and sold in 1889 to J. Read of Portsmouth to be broken up.

The Figurehead

The story of Actaeon the huntsman records that, while out hunting deer, he came across Diana, the huntress queen, who was bathing in a woodland pool with her nymphs. Annoyed at being discovered, Diana turned Actaeon into a stag. He was then chased by his huntsman friends and was eventually torn to pieces by his own hounds.

The figurehead has no obvious allusions to Actaeon the hunter but in all probability these would have appeared in the carvings that would have flowed down onto the trailboards below the figurehead (see *Eurydice* on page 64 for an example of trailboard carvings). The identity of this figurehead is not, however, in any doubt as the 1911 Admiralty Catalogue included him in the Portsmouth collection, stating that he had been presented by Mr John Read, whose company had broken up the ship. See also Ships' Badges on page 96.

National Museum of the Royal Navy.

Royal Adelaide – 1833-1877

Yacht, 50bm, 50ft

The Vessel

Not to be confused with the 1828 HMS *Royal Adelaide* – a 1st Rate ship of the line of 104 guns – this was a miniature frigate used on royal occasions on Virginia Water, Surrey. Both vessels were named after Queen Adelaide, the wife of King William IV, but the yacht was modelled on a frigate then building in Plymouth Yard, HMS *Pique*.

The *Royal Adelaide* was built at Sheerness Dockyard in 1833 before being dismantled and transported to Virginia Water where in May 1834 she was launched with great ceremony. The King had said that the public should witness the event and several thousand attended, marshalled by Life Guards and Foot Guards with a band of the former playing from a boat moored on the lake. When the King and Queen arrived there were numerous gun salutes while they were rowed by six scarlet-coated watermen in the royal barge, first to the slipway, where the yacht was named, and then to the *Superb*, the favourite royal fishing boat, from which they witnessed the launch.

The yacht had all the outward appearance of a thirty-six-gun frigate and had twenty-two brass guns mounted for ceremonial gun salutes. Her cabin was spacious, measuring 16 x 14ft, so it is not surprising that Queen Victoria's children enjoyed being sailed round the lake in her.

HMS *Pique*. From *Sailing Ships of War 1800–1860* by Sir Alan Moore.

She was broken up in 1877 and her armament was presented to the Royal Yacht Squadron at Cowes.

The Figurehead

One of the smallest figureheads in the collection, this three-quarter-length representation of Queen Adelaide was carved by Robert Hall, carver, of Rotherhithe. There must have been a mass of other carved work and gilding as the estimate submitted by Robert Hall in December 1833 for all the carved work was for £78.0.0 – much more than such a small figurehead would have justified – and the Surveyor of the Navy approved the figure!

It would appear that the figurehead was initially taken into the Plymouth collection as it was recorded as being there in the 1911 Admiralty Catalogue. However, in July 1914 King George V made an unexpected visit to the Portsmouth Dockyard Museum and commanded that the *Royal Adelaide* figurehead should be displayed there. While not being included in the 1914 edition of the Museum catalogue, it does feature in the 1919 edition.

HMS *Blazer* – 1834-1853

Paddle gunvessel, 527bm, 145ft

The Ship

Built in Chatham Dockyard and launched there in May 1834, she was the third ship to be named *Blazer*, the first of the name having been one of a group of gunboats built in the 1790s. With names such as *Boxer*, *Blazer* and *Bruiser*, it is claimed that these vessels were named after a pack of hounds, the First Sea Lord at the time being a keen huntsman! Classed initially as a steam vessel, she and her sister ship were re-classed in 1844 as first class steam gunvessels. Paddle driven and armed with only three guns, she is the smallest warship represented in the Portsmouth figurehead collection, being only 145ft long.

It was suggested in some early correspondence within the journal of The Society for Nautical Research that, because the Commanding Officer of HMS *Blazer* is said to have dressed his ship's company in uniform blue and white striped guernseys, these were named 'blazers' and it is in them that the modern sporting jacket has its origin. This theory is disputed by etymologists who argue that the earliest blazers were made of material of the brightest possible scarlet – hence the name.

HMS *Blazer* saw service in the Mediterranean and on the North America and West Indies Station before undertaking surveying duties in the North Sea. She was taken to pieces in Portsmouth Dockyard in 1853.

The Figurehead

Admiralty records of 1834 show that the figurehead carver, Robert Hall of Rotherhithe, submitted no less than five designs for the figurehead from which the Surveyor of the Navy could choose. Unfortunately, the designs have not survived but he was allowed £6.10.0 for his efforts and the most unusual representation of the blazing sun resulted. Perhaps because it was not recognised as a typical figurehead, the carving does not appear in the 1911 Admiralty Catalogue, even though it is included in the 1911 edition of the Portsmouth Museum catalogue.

> ### BATTLE HONOURS
>
> Battle Honours are granted to HM Ships and Fleet Air Arm squadrons that have taken part in certain actions or campaigns. The system was first formalised in 1954 when a list was published by the Admiralty, the first honour being 'ARMADA 1588'. Each ship and squadron has a teak 'scroll' on which the ship's badge and all honours awarded to ships of that name are recorded, the intention being to foster esprit de corps amongst the officers and ship's company and to encourage an interest in past war-time exploits.
>
> As the focus of this book is the ship's figurehead and therefore the places and actions it might have 'seen' during its period of service, the Battle Honours included in these pages are only those granted to that figurehead's particular ship and not those granted to other ships of the same name.

HMS *Cleopatra* – 1835-1862

6th Rate, 26 guns, 918bm, 130ft
Battle Honour: Burma 1853

The Ship

As seen below in the description of the figurehead, the identity of this carving has been in some doubt during part of its life. Always assuming that it did come originally from the 1835 *Cleopatra*, she was built at Pembroke Dock and was launched there in April 1835, a 6th Rate and only the second ship of that name.

She saw service ranging between the South American Station, the North American and West Indies Station – where she was involved in anti-slave trade operations – and in the East Indies – where she was granted her Battle Honour 'Burma 1853'.

She returned to Chatham in 1855 where she was decommissioned and was sold to Castle & Beech for breaking up in 1862.

The Figurehead

Cleopatra's figurehead was carved by Robert Hall of Princes Stairs, Rotherhithe, for which he was allowed £6.10.0, although there was much discussion about its actual delivery, with heated letters being exchanged on the subject between the Surveyor of the Navy and the Superintendent at Woolwich.

When the ship was broken up the figurehead was preserved in the Chatham collection where it was included in the 1911 Admiralty Catalogue. There was, however, some confusion over which carving had come from the *Cleopatra* and which from the *Gleaner* of 1833. By the time the 1948 muster of figureheads was conducted, the doubt seems to have been resolved and this figurehead was reported as being in the small collection at HMS *Ganges*, the boys' training establishment at Shotley, Suffolk, complete with a photograph and

a caption saying 'HMS *Cleopatra* from Chatham'. After training ceased at Shotley, this figurehead – amongst others – was transferred to the National Museum of the Royal Navy, arriving in 1984.

OTHER FIGUREHEAD COLLECTIONS
CHATHAM

As with the other royal dockyards, the Chatham collection of figureheads was the by-product of the ship-breaking activity there. By 1911 when the Admiralty Catalogue was compiled, there were no fewer than fifty in the collection, most of which were housed in a Dockyard Museum.

In 1913, the Honorary Secretary of the Society for Nautical Research, Douglas Owen, wrote several articles in the society's journal, *The Mariner's Mirror*, following a tour of the royal dockyards. He described the most important figureheads in the dockyard collections in much more detail, selecting thirteen of the Chatham collection for this review.

During the 1930s and 1940s there was a trend to place the figureheads where they could more easily be seen and many were grouped in the vicinity of the Admiral Superintendent's house and beside an avenue called 'Admiral's Walk'. In the years before and after the dockyard's closure in 1984, some of the figureheads were dispersed to naval establishments, some reached the National Maritime Museum at Greenwich and only about a dozen remained in the area. Since then the Historic Dockyard has acquired several more that were in need of restoration and the collection is steadily growing.

HMS *Trafalgar* – 1841-1873

1st Rate, 120 guns, 2,404bm, 196ft
Battle Honour: Crimea 1854

The Ship

Built in Woolwich Dockyard as a 1st Rate ship and launched there in 1841 after eleven years on the stocks, she was employed as flagship to the Commander-in-Chief of Sheerness and then saw service in the Crimean War, taking part in the bombardment of Sebastopol.

In 1858 she was cut down from a three-decker to a two-decker, was converted to steam and emerged in 1859 as an eighty-nine-gun 'screw battleship'. She served in both the Channel and Mediterranean Fleets before becoming the guardship at Queensferry in 1865. In 1870 she became a sea-going training ship for cadets but by 1873 she was permanently stationed at Portland as a boys' training ship and was renamed *Boscawen*. She was sold in 1906 to Castle & Co. of London for breaking up.

The Figurehead

Several alternative designs were offered for the figurehead in 1836 when the ship was building at Woolwich. Hellyer & Browning of Rotherhithe submitted the design shown here (£31.10.0) with another in the form of a full-length

winged figure of 'Fame' blowing her trumpet (£42.0.0). Robert Hall, also of Rotherhithe, forwarded a simple bust in loose robes (£45.0.0). None appear to have been accepted; probably because of the long delays in the ship's construction.

In 1840 Hellyer & Son of Portsmouth Yard submitted another design with an estimate for £45.0.0 based on a bust of Lord Nelson that the Surveyor of the Navy had purchased in London. While the figurehead design has not survived, it is almost certainly the one we know today as in 1843 Hellyer & Son charged £5.15.0 for 'Altering the Figure Head in consequence of the Bowsprit touching the Hat…'

When the ship was sold for breaking up, the figurehead was added to the small collection at HMS *Ganges* – the boys' training establishment at Shotley, Suffolk. He remained there until 1976 when *Ganges* closed and Lord Nelson came to Portsmouth. He is shown wearing round his neck the gold medal presented to him after the Battle of St Vincent in 1797 and on his left breast the stars of the Order of the Crescent (Turkey), the Order of St Ferdinand (Naples and Sicily) and the Order of the Bath.

Design by Hellyer & Browning dated 1836.
(TNA – ADM 87/6)

HMS *Eurydice* – 1843-1878

6th Rate, 24 guns, 908bm, 141ft

The Ship

Built in Portsmouth Dockyard, and launched there in May 1843, she was the second ship of the name. She served in the White Sea during the war with Russia but it is her tragic end for which she is chiefly remembered. She had become a sea training ship for boy seamen in 1861 and was returning from a cruise to the West Indies in 1878 when she was struck by a squall off the Isle of Wight and capsized. Over 300 lives were lost and there were only two survivors.

She lay in water less than 50ft deep so that her masts and upper spars were visible above the surface. After several false starts, divers managed to attach ropes to her hull that were then secured to HM Ships *Pearl* and *Rinaldo* at low tide. As the tide rose, so did the *Eurydice* and she was towed into shallower water before she was finally raised. She was taken to Portsmouth to be taken to pieces, her figurehead being passed to the Dockyard Museum for preservation.

Design by J.E. Hellyer dated 1842.
(TNA – ADM 87/12)

The Figurehead

Eurydice was the wife of Orpheus, the supreme minstrel of Greek mythology who played the lyre so beautifully that the whole of nature would listen entranced. One day Eurydice trod on a snake, was bitten and she died. Orpheus was heartbroken and found the passage to the Underworld where he charmed with his music Charon, the ferryman, Cerberus, the watchdog, and also Hades, god of the dead and ruler of the underworld. Because of his music he was allowed to recover Eurydice providing he did not look back until he reached the upper air again. With the end of the tunnel in sight, Orpheus could not resist gazing at his wife's face. Having broken his promise, Eurydice was turned into a wraith of mist.

The figurehead was carved by J.E. Hellyer, the resident carver at Portsmouth, for which he was allowed £18.0.0. He carved Eurydice reaching out for her husband with a look of despair on her face.

The trailboard carvings that complemented the figurehead have not survived but can be seen on the design that was submitted for approval by the Admiral Superintendent at Portsmouth in December 1842. They tell the rest of the story; a little imp grasps her dress to pull her back, while the snake that bit her makes good its escape.

Black Eagle – 1842-1876

Admiralty Yacht

Formerly HMS Firebrand *1831-1842*
Paddle Gunvessel, 6 x 9pdr carronades

The Ship

Built as HMS *Firebrand* by Curling, Young & Co. of Limehouse and launched there in July 1831, she was initially classed as a steam vessel being powered through paddle-wheels from a 'Butterley' engine. In 1833 she was re-engined with a 'Maudslay' engine and in 1835 was used by the Admiralty Board to tour the royal dockyards.

In 1842 she was renamed *Black Eagle* in honour of the Prussian royal family, who frequently cruised in her, and she became the Admiralty Yacht. This was a period of much technical development and to fulfil her role she was lengthened, given three masts, two funnels and engines with extra power. In 1857 she became a tender in Portsmouth Harbour and was taken to pieces there in 1876.

The Figurehead

There is some evidence that the original figurehead for HMS *Firebrand* was carved by George Faldo of London for an estimated cost of £24.12.8 but the design is not described. The letter books of the Comptroller and Surveyor of the Navy for 1842 note that the approval for the carved work for the *Black Eagle* did not pass through that office – presumably because an Admiralty Yacht did not require the full authorisation process normally applied to one of Her Majesty's ships. Despite this, there was an exchange of letters in 1846 in which the Admiral Superintendent at Portsmouth was invited to direct Mr Hellyer, the carver, to propose a figurehead forthwith for the *Black Eagle*. Clearly the Surveyor of the Navy was becoming impatient with the delays and it may be assumed that it was Mr Hellyer who carved the figurehead in the form of an eagle.

The eagle has the Prussian crown carved on its breast and its wings carry the same markings as were on the Prussian royal coat of arms.

After the ship was taken to pieces, the figurehead stood for some years in the garden of Admiralty House, Portsmouth, until the first curator of the Dockyard Museum, Mr Mark Frost, managed to have it brought under cover in the museum. It was included in the first Museum catalogue of 1911.

National Maritime Museum PAH8662.

Princess Alice – 1844-1878

Iron paddle packet, 270bm, 140ft

The Ship

Designed by Thomas Ditchburn and built by Ditchburn & Mare of Blackwall as a steam mail packet, she was launched there in 1843. Powered by a Maudslay steam engine and driven by paddle-wheels, she had sleek lines, two raked masts and a tall stovepipe funnel.

She was purchased by the Admiralty in 1844 and her name must have been chosen in honour of Queen Victoria's third child, Princess Alice Maud Mary, who had been born at Buckingham Palace the year before. She was based in Dover as part of the packet service providing a cross-Channel mail and passenger service.

In 1864 she became the tender to HMS *Royal Adelaide*, the flagship at Devonport, and so was used as the Commander-in-Chief's yacht. She was taken to pieces in Devonport Dockyard in 1878.

National Museum of the Royal Navy.

The Figurehead

Only 3ft in length, *Princess Alice* is one of the smallest figureheads in the collection but she is widely travelled.

In the 1911 Admiralty Catalogue she is listed amongst sixty-eight figureheads at Devonport Dockyard where she is described as 'Paddle Yacht, wood, built at Blackwall 1843. Attached to Devonport for the Commander-in-Chief, and broken up 1878.'

In 1913 and 1914 The Society for Nautical Research included articles in its journal, *The Mariner's Mirror*, that described the dockyard figurehead collections. *Princess Alice* was recorded as being in the Fire-Engine House in Devonport Dockyard: 'Bust of a young woman inclining forward, very pretty face. Brown bodice with red rose at breast opening' (clearly she has had a change of clothing since 1914!). When the figureheads were mustered in the late 1930s she was still in the Fire-Engine House but an intention was stated to move her to the RN Barracks.

By 1957 she had moved to Malta and was recorded as being one of four figureheads in a list submitted by the Admiral Superintendent there, she being in the entrance to the Wardroom of HMS *Phoenicia*, a shore establishment on Manoel Island.

As part of the Royal Navy's withdrawal from Malta in the early 1970s, the four resident figureheads were shipped home to the UK and were added to the Portsmouth collection. (See also HMS *Caradoc*, HMS *Cruizer* and HMS *Hibernia*.)

HMS *Grampus* – 1845-1897

4th Rate, 50 guns

Formerly HMS Tremendous *1784-1845*
3rd Rate, 74 guns, 1,656bm, 170ft
Battle Honours: First of June 1794, Cape of Good Hope 1795

The Ship

Built as HMS *Tremendous* by William Barnard of Deptford and launched there in 1784, she saw action in 1794 at The Glorious First of June as part of Admiral Lord Howe's fleet and in 1795 at the Battle of the Cape of Good Hope under Vice Admiral Sir George Elphinstone.

Between 1807 and 1811 she was reconstructed at Chatham incorporating a design of diagonal frames. In 1845 she was 'cut down' at Woolwich to convert her to a single gun-deck frigate and was renamed HMS *Grampus*.

Many of the wooden-wall ships were used for accommodation or storage after their seagoing days were over. In 1856, *Grampus* became a powder depot at Portsmouth and in 1883 a War Department powder depot. She was eventually sold to be broken up by J. Read of Portsmouth in 1897.

The Figurehead

During her long period of service, she had several figureheads. It is known that George Williams of Chatham carved a replacement figurehead for HMS *Tremendous* in 1810 but neither the details of this nor the original have survived. When the ship was cut down, a replacement would also have been needed to fit the smaller bow structure. Hellyer & Son, the resident carvers of Portsmouth Dockyard, submitted the design shown below in March 1845.

The ship was still being referred to as *Tremendous* and it was therefore appropriate to have Hercules as the figurehead wearing his protective lion skin with his club in the trailboards. By June that year, however, it was decided that the name *Tremendous* was no longer suitable for a 4th Rate ship and she was renamed *Grampus* – a member of the dolphin family. The Hellyers were instructed to design a figurehead that was more appropriate for the new name and carved one to represent Neptune. Drawings of the ship being broken up in 1897 show the Neptune figure on the bow.

Design by Hellyer & Son dated 1845.
(TNA – ADM 87/15)

Fairy – 1845-1868

Iron steam yacht, 312bm, 145ft

The Vessel

Built on the Thames by Ditchburn & Mare of Blackwall and launched there in March 1845, she was an iron screw yacht designed to complement the Royal Yacht *Victoria and Albert*. With a shallow draught and a narrow beam, she could navigate the rivers of the West Country and squeeze through the locks of the Caledonian Canal that were otherwise inaccessible to Queen Victoria during her royal cruises. The Queen also used the *Fairy* to boost the morale of her fleet, steaming amongst the ships anchored at Spithead before they sailed to the Baltic in March 1854.

She had to be able to keep up with the Royal Yacht's 11 knots and *The Illustrated London News* reported with delight that, during trials on the measured mile at Long-Reach, 'her speed was found to be 15mph, which is the greatest rate a vessel has ever been propelled by a screw.'

The name *Fairy* had previously been used for three naval brig-sloops and the Celtic 'airy spirit' was appropriate for this little craft. She served Queen Victoria well for almost twenty years before she was replaced by the *Alberta* – see Appendix II. She was broken up in Portsmouth Dockyard in 1868.

The Figurehead

With the yacht being built on the Thames, it is surprising that the figurehead was not carved there as well. No design drawings exist for this carving but the Admiral Superintendent at Portsmouth forwarded in July 1846 an estimate for £4.15.0 for carved work on the *Fairy* and, as this sum is about the right value for a small figurehead, it was probably carved by J.E. Hellyer of Portsmouth as a late addition. She is a simple three-quarter-length female bust that would have fitted neatly under the yacht's bowsprit.

After the yacht was broken up, the figurehead was preserved in the dockyard at Portsmouth and appeared in the first edition of the Dockyard Museum's catalogue in 1911.

HMS *Calypso* — 1845-1866

6th Rate, 20 guns, 731bm, 120ft

The Ship

Built in Chatham Dockyard and launched in 1845, she was a 6th Rate of twenty guns. In her first commission she saw service in the Pacific visiting the Pitcairn Islands and Tahiti and punishing the natives of Fiji for earlier acts of aggression against some of the white residents. In the 1850s she served on the North America and West Indies Station before returning to the Pacific. She was broken up in 1866 by Castle & Beech at Charlton.

The Figurehead

In Greek mythology, Calypso was a sea-nymph who lived on the mythical island of Ogygia on which Odysseus was shipwrecked when returning home from Troy, keeping him there for seven years before allowing him to continue his journey.

Design by Hellyer & Son dated 1843. (TNA – ADM 87/13)

In July 1843, the Captain Superintendent at Chatham forwarded the above design that can be seen to incorporate allusions to the sea; the shell on her head and the bulrushes surrounding her waist. The notation 'Appd.' to the left of the nymph's head shows that the design was approved even though the carver's estimate of £12 in his covering letter was not agreed; only £8.18.0 being allowed.

The *Calypso* figurehead was preserved at Chatham and is listed there in the 1911 Admiralty Catalogue. She was also described in an article in *The Mariner's Mirror* of 1913 as:

CALYPSO – A well-developed female bust to the waist; a smirking expression on a well satisfied, rather pretty face. Waving hair in Grecian style; a long curl descending to the breast on either side. A black bead necklace, apparently oak-galls, graduated on a loose wire, with small black Latin cross as a pendant. Loose brass ear-rings; below the waist a small lyre.

And so she appeared when she was photographed for the return sent from Chatham to the Admiralty in 1938.

When next photographed ten years later, and after she had been transferred to HMS *Ganges* in Suffolk, she had lost her necklace and had been given a 'robe' to cover her left breast. It is not recorded whether this was added to cover up damage to the carving or as a display of modesty in the training establishment for boy seamen! On the closure of HMS *Ganges*, she was transferred to the Portsmouth collection where she has retained her recently acquired 'wooden' robe. The bulrushes that were incorporated in the Hellyer design over 150 years ago can still be seen.

HMS *Caradoc* – 1847-1870

Iron Paddle Packet, 676bm, 193ft
Battle Honour: Crimea 1854-55

The Ship

An iron paddle gunboat built by Ditchburn & Mare of Blackwall and launched in 1847, she served first as a Mail Packet based on Holyhead. She was the first ship of this name to serve in the Royal Navy and *British Warship Names* attributes it to one of the Knights of the Round Table, Caradoc being the English name for Caractacus. Other sources suggest that he was the Welsh leader against the Roman invasion in AD 43.

During the Crimean War she was based in the Black Sea where she earned her Battle Honour 'Crimea 1854–55'. After the death of the commander of the British troops, Field Marshal Lord Raglan, in July 1855 from dysentery, the honour of bringing his body home was given to HMS *Caradoc*. It was transferred at the mouth of the Avon to the steamer *Star* who carried it to Bristol.

From 1858 to 1868 *Caradoc* served in the Mediterranean, much of the time being based in Malta. She returned to Portsmouth in 1869 and was sold in 1870 to E. Bates for breaking up.

The Figurehead

The figurehead gives little indication of what the carver was trying to portray as the carving does not appear to represent either the king of an ancient Welsh tribe or a knight of the Round Table! Perhaps the trailboard carvings would have provided the clue but, unfortunately, neither these nor a design sketch have survived.

What happened to the figurehead when the ship was broken up in 1870 is not clear as it was not listed in the 1911 Admiralty Catalogue. It did, however, find its way to Malta, presumably because of the ship's connection with the island during her service career. In the 1957 muster, the Flag Officer Malta reported him as being 'Lascar – ex-HMS *Caradoc*, being at the Lascaris Bastion.' The Lascaris Bastion is an ancient fortification beside Grand Harbour that was for many years the Headquarters of the Commander-in-Chief of the Mediterranean and thus an appropriate place for the preservation of such a relic.

Perhaps it was this association with seamen from India that resulted in him being painted with a black face, for this was his colour when he returned to Portsmouth in 1983. He stood for some years with the figurehead of HMS *Cruizer* at the entrance to the parade area beside HMS *Victory* but was removed to store when that area was redeveloped. It is hoped to have both figureheads displayed again with the next round of museum developments.

RATES OF SHIPS

Warships of the sailing navies were divided into six 'Rates' according to the number of guns carried. The precise division between the rates varied over the centuries but, in simple terms, 1st, 2nd and 3rd Rate ships all had sufficient guns to be able to take part in the line of battle; 1st Rates having 100 guns or more while 3rd Rates had between sixty and eighty guns. 4th, 5th and 6th Rates had fewer guns, the last two categories being generally known as frigates.

Paddle Yacht, 98bm

The Vessel

Built in Chatham Dockyard and launched there in 1849, she was a paddle yacht built as a tender to the first Royal Yacht *Victoria and Albert* – see Appendix II.

Powered by two 20hp engines, her main use was as a dispatch boat carrying papers for the royal household between Osborne House on the Isle of Wight and Portsmouth or Southampton, thus acquiring the local name of 'the milk boat'. She was broken up at Portsmouth in 1901.

The Figurehead

The sketch below shows the design that was drawn by Hellyer & Son of Portsmouth on an outline provided by Chatham Yard in November 1848. The Hellyer estimate for carving the full-length figure was £20; the design and cost being accepted by the Surveyor of the Navy.

Why there was a change of heart is not clear from the Admiralty records but in October 1849 Hellyer & Son forwarded an estimate for £5 for 'a neat busthead' and it was in this form that the figurehead was installed. She was included in the first catalogue of the Portsmouth Dockyard Museum in 1911.

National Museum of the Royal Navy.

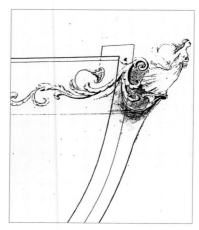

Design by Hellyer & Son dated 1848. (TNA – ADM 87/24)

Unknown Lady – c.1850

Brig-sloop, 10 guns, 237bm, 90ft

The Vessel

As may be implied from her description, the origin of this figurehead is not known but she is very much in the style and of a weight that would suit the bow of a mid-nineteenth-century frigate.

The Figurehead

The figurehead is carved as a three-quarter-length female bust with her right breast exposed from a loose-fitting dress and wearing a wreath made from bulrushes. The bulrush has been used as a symbol of faithfulness and humility and was probably put there by the carver as a form of identity. Perhaps she represents a character from Greek or Roman mythology or maybe a more modern name that would have been explained in the trailboard carvings. Unfortunately these have not survived.

The fact that she was included in the 1911 Catalogue of the Portsmouth Dockyard Museum suggests that the ship was taken to pieces in the dockyard before that date but that does not narrow down the field sufficiently to guess from what ship she came.

As with the other royal dockyards, the Devonport collection of figureheads was the bi-product of the ship-breaking activity there. The original collection was housed in a building called the Adelaide Gallery but it was destroyed by fire in September 1840 as were the historic artefacts. As more ships were taken to pieces, the collection again grew and, when the 1911 Admiralty Catalogue was compiled, there were sixty-five named figureheads housed in various buildings around the yard.

In 1913 and 1914, the Honorary Secretary of the Society for Nautical Research, Douglas Owen, wrote several articles in the society's journal, The Mariner's Mirror, in which he described the most important figureheads in the collection in much more detail, selecting no less than forty-four of the Devonport collection for this review.

In 1936 when the National Maritime Museum was being formed at Greenwich, the Admiralty gave nineteen figureheads from the Devonport collection as part of its contribution to the core collection there. During the Second World War, Devonport Dockyard was heavily bombed and nine more figureheads were lost.

The post-war years saw a policy of allocating figureheads to naval establishments to encourage an interest in naval history but recent years have seen some of these returning to the small museum in the South Yard. The present collection has been consolidated in one of the ropery buildings of the South Yard where there is an impressive display of sixteen figureheads.

HMS *Cruizer* – 1852-1912

Wood screw sloop, 752bm, 960 tons, 160ft
Battle Honour: Baltic 1854–55

The Ship

Built in Deptford Dockyard and launched in 1852, she was the tenth ship of the name; a wood screw sloop armed with seventeen 32-pounder guns. She took part in the bombardment of Helsinki in 1855 and then transferred to the China Station taking part in the Battle of Fatshan Creek in 1857. Also in 1857 her name was changed to HMS *Cruizer* and under this name she continued to operate in Chinese waters, surveying the Gulf of Pechili and preparing the moorings for the Allied fleet that was to disembark troops for the advance on Peking.

She returned to England and was laid up until 1867 when she was re-commissioned for the Mediterranean Station. Here in 1872 – and having had her guns and engine removed – she became a sail-training ship intended to give young officers and ratings experience in sailing square-rigged ships. In 1893 she was renamed HMS *Lark* and remained in service until early in the twentieth century. She was sold in 1912 and was broken up in Malta.

The Figurehead

The design sketch below was drawn by the figurehead carvers Hellyer & Son of Blackwall and forwarded to the Surveyor of the Navy in October 1851. The carver offered either a Demi Head – as shown – for £9.10.0 or a Bust Head – without arms – for £6.10.0.

The Surveyor chose the cheaper alternative, showing his decision on the sketch by drawing lines across each of the sailor's arms. Having lost the sailor's hat with his right arm, the carver naturally put it on his head where it remains today.

When the ship was broken up, the figurehead was landed in Malta and remained there for many years. He survived the bombing in 1942, even though the fort in which he was housed was badly damaged, and was returned to Portsmouth when the navy withdrew from Malta in 1978. He stood for some years with the figurehead of HMS *Caradoc* at the entrance to the parade area beside HMS *Victory* but was removed to store when that area was redeveloped. It is hoped to have both figureheads displayed again with the next round of museum developments.

Design by Hellyer & Son dated 1851. (TNA – ADM 87/38)

H.M.S. CRUIZER

HMS *Malacca* – 1853-1906

Wood screw sloop, 1,034bm, 192ft

The Ship

Originally ordered in May 1841 to be built by the East India Company in Bombay, the order was suspended in October that year and it was not until October 1848 that the order was given that she was to be built as a screw ship in Moulmein, Burma. Built of teak, she was launched there in April 1853 but she had to be sailed back to Chatham for her engines to be fitted.

In the mid-1850s she saw service in the Mediterranean and then in the North America and West Indies Station. She was commissioned again in 1861 and saw service first in the Mediterranean and then in the Pacific.

She was sold in 1869 for breaking up but was re-sold to the Japanese Navy to serve as *Tsukuba*. She was finally broken up in 1906.

The Figurehead

In the summer of 1844 the figurehead carvers at Portsmouth – Hellyer & Son – wrote to the Surveyor of the Navy in London telling him that work was slack and asking that an order should be placed for the carved work for the ships that were being built in Bombay. The request was successful as he was instructed to submit designs for HM Ships *Madras*, *Malacca*, *Zebra* and *Goshawk* – 'observing that they are to be made characteristic of the country in which they are building.'

The design below is that which was submitted for HMS *Malacca* and was approved; the carver being allowed £9.0.0 for his efforts.

It is not known whether the Hellyer figurehead ever reached Moulmein or whether it was actually fitted to the ship. Certainly the carving that is now in the Portsmouth collection is not the same but there could be an explanation for that. Perhaps it was carved when the ship returned to Chatham for her engines to be fitted or perhaps a replacement was needed as a result of damage. The Admiralty records at The National Archives do not provide any clues. Whatever the reason, he is a beautiful example of the carver's art.

Design by Hellyer & Son dated 1844.
(TNA – ADM 87/14)

HMS *Wanderer* — 1855-1866

Wood screw gunvessel, 675bm, 181ft

The Ship

Built on the Thames by R. & H. Green of Blackwall and launched there in November 1855, HMS *Wanderer* was a second class gunvessel of the Vigilant Class. Several classes of shallow draught vessels of this type were built to meet the need for inshore operations in the Baltic and Black Seas in the war with Russia. With a wooden hull, she was propeller driven from a Maudslay, Sons & Field single-expansion steam engine and was armed with four guns of various sizes.

She did not see any war service but did spend much of her relatively short life in the Mediterranean. She was sold to Castles of Charlton in August 1866 for breaking up.

The Figurehead

R. & H. Green were building three gunvessels of the Vigilant Class; *Assurance*, *Coquette* and *Wanderer* and in September 1855 forwarded a figurehead design for each with a request for early approval as *Coquette* was to be launched the following month. The designs were approved three days later and the drawings returned. As no costs were mentioned in the correspondence, these would have been included in the ship contract and local carvers would have been employed.

Before *Wanderer* was sold for breaking up, the figurehead was taken into the Chatham Dockyard collection and was listed as being there in the 1911 Admiralty Catalogue. In the 1940s it was amongst those that were moved outside to line the Admiral's Walk and there it remained until 1974 when it was transferred to the National Museum of the Royal Navy at Portsmouth.

OTHER FIGUREHEAD COLLECTIONS
THE NATIONAL MARITIME MUSEUM

Unlike the figurehead collections in the royal dockyards that arose from their ship-breaking activities, the collection in the National Maritime Museum at Greenwich has its origin in a gift by the Lords of the Admiralty in 1936 prior to the museum's official opening in April 1937.

Nineteen large and historically significant figureheads were selected from the Devonport collection and were transferred to Greenwich where many of them were displayed in Neptune's Hall. Others have joined them over the years from such places as Chatham Dockyard, the Royal United Services Institute and from private collections. There are now almost forty in the collection but of these only about one third are at present on show, although others are in display condition and can be loaned or included in appropriate temporary exhibitions.

HMS *Peterel* – 1860-1901

Wooden screw sloop, 11 guns, 669bm, 160ft

The Ship

Built in Devonport Dockyard and launched there in November 1860, she was one of the Rosario Class of third class sloops, several of which were named after birds; the petrel being associated with St Peter as it hovers over the sea with its legs hanging down, thus giving the appearance of walking on water.

HMS *Peterel* saw service on the North America and West Indies Station in her first commission and on the Cape of Good Hope Station, both on the east and west coasts of Africa, in her second. She served in the Pacific in the mid-1870s and finally she was used as a lightship to mark the wreck of HMS *Vanguard* which had sunk off the coast of Ireland when in collision with HMS *Iron Duke* in September 1875. In 1885 *Peterel* was reduced to a coal hulk and was sold in 1901.

The Figurehead

The figurehead is a simple three-quarter-length female bust with a petrel in the trailboards, carved by the resident carver at Devonport, Frederick Dickerson.

When the ship was sold, the figurehead was preserved in Devonport Dockyard and was recorded as being there in the 1911 Admiralty Catalogue. In the 1940s she was displayed by the cricket pitch at the RN Barracks where she survived the Blitz but, by the 1957 muster of figureheads, she had been moved to HMS *Royal Arthur*, a leadership training establishment near Corsham, Wiltshire. She was later transferred to the Ministry of Defence offices at Foxhill, Bath, and it was from there that she was rescued by the Portsmouth Royal Dockyard Historical Trust who now own her and have had her restored.

She is not part of the National Museum of the Royal Navy collection but can be found in Boathouse No.7 amongst the displays of 'The Dockyard Apprentice' exhibition.

Design by Frederick Dickerson of Devonport dated 1860. (Private Collection)

HMS *Warrior* – 1860

Armoured iron frigate, 6,109bm, 9,210 tons, 380ft

The Ship

Built by Thames Ironworks Co. of Blackwall and launched there in December 1860, she was of a revolutionary design intended to counter the threat of the French armoured ship *Gloire* that had been launched the previous year. Classed initially as a frigate, *Warrior* was the second ship of the name – see the earlier HMS *Warrior* of 1781 – and was the Royal Navy's first iron-hulled, armoured seagoing warship. She was armed with forty guns, both muzzle-loaders and breech-loaders, and propelled by sails and a single screw powered by a two-cylinder single-expansion steam engine.

Warrior served in the Channel Fleet conducting trials, cruising right round Britain to show herself off to the public and travelling as far south as Gibraltar. She did not, however, get involved in any actions. In 1871 she entered a four-year refit and then joined the First Reserve Squadron, a role that involved enrolling and drilling members of the Royal Naval Reserve and the Coastguard, and taking part in annual summer cruises. In 1881 she was re-classed as an armoured cruiser. 1883 saw the end of her sea-going career and she served variously as a depot ship for Portsmouth destroyers, a floating workshop and powerhouse for the Naval Torpedo School, HMS *Vernon*, losing her name in 1916. When the Torpedo School moved ashore, the remains of *Warrior* became a mooring hulk for oil tankers at Pembroke Dock in South Wales where she remained for a further fifty years.

On the closure of the oil fuel depot in 1976 and after much negotiating, *Warrior* was given to The Maritime Trust and taken to Hartlepool

From *Sailing Ships of War 1800-1860* by Sir Alan Moore.

for a complete reconstruction and preparation for public display, arriving at the Portsmouth Historic Dockyard in June 1987.

The Figurehead

The design of *Warrior*'s first figurehead was approved in August 1860 and was carved by the Hellyer family of Rotherhithe, probably in the form of a Saracen with a scimitar. It was lost when *Warrior* and HMS *Royal Oak* were in collision in August 1868, and the Hellyers carved a replacement, this time with a more traditional warrior and short sword. That figurehead came ashore when the ship was being modified to become part of the Naval Torpedo School and he was displayed inside the dockyard main gate from 1900 to 1963, slowly deteriorating and being patched up. In 1963 the Home Fleet headquarters at Northwood, Middlesex, had been named HMS *Warrior* and the Commander-in-Chief asked for the figurehead to be relocated there. This was done but it was not long before the rot had spread so far that it was condemned and destroyed.

When the ship was being reconstructed at Hartlepool, a third figurehead was commissioned, this one being carved between 1981 and 1983 by Jack Whitehead and Norman Gaches at Wootton on the Isle of Wight. It is this carving that can be seen on the bow of *Warrior* today.

HMS *Centurion* – 1892-1910

Battleship, 10,500 tons, 360ft
Battle Honour: China 1900

The Ship

Built in Portsmouth Dockyard and launched in 1892, she was one of two second class battleships designed for operation in the Far East with heavier guns than the Russian armoured cruisers on the Pacific Station and yet with a shallow draught to allow navigation of the Chinese rivers. Her sister ship was HMS *Barfleur* whose figurehead is included in Appendix III.

After a period of trials, she commissioned in Portsmouth early in 1894 to become the flagship of the China Station. From 1897 to 1900 she was engaged in allied operations in north China during the Boxer Rebellion. Her landing parties with the naval brigades stormed the Taku forts and relieved the Tientsin legations.

She returned to Portsmouth in 1901 for an extensive refit that included the removal of her figurehead – a decoration that no longer seemed appropriate in the early years of the twentieth century.

The Figurehead

Carved in the form of a bearded and armoured warrior, this figurehead is unique in the collection in that he was designed to stand bolt upright as can be seen in the photograph of HMS *Centurion* in dock.

Once removed from the ship in 1901, the figurehead was transferred to the dockyard and was included in the first edition of the Dockyard Museum's catalogue in 1911.

National Museum of the Royal Navy.

92

HMS *Espiegle* – 1900-1923

Sloop, 1,070 tons, 185ft
Battle Honour: Mesopotamia 1914-16

The Ship

Built in Sheerness Dockyard and launched in 1900, she was the seventh ship to bear the name, the first being the French brig *L'Espiègle* captured in 1794 off Ushant. As was the custom with ships that had been captured from other nations and had not been re-named, when they came to the end of their useful life, another warship was named after them. The 1900 *Espiegle* was a steel screw sloop armed with six 4in guns and four 3-pounders. She was one of six Cadmus Class sloops that were the last ships of the Royal Navy to retain in their design an element of sail power, and she was the last Royal Navy ship afloat and in commission to carry a figurehead.

She served on the China Station from 1902 to 1904 and as a training ship at Dartmouth from 1905 to 1910. In 1914 she operated in the Persian Gulf supporting the British Expeditionary Force and was involved in a number of skirmishes including the capture of a Turkish fort at Fao and the sinking of a Turkish motorboat at Shatt-el-Arab, being granted the Battle Honour 'Mesopotamia 1914–16'. She was sold at Bombay in 1923.

The Figurehead

With a name that had its origins in the French *L'Espiègle*, her Edwardian ship's company must have had difficulty understanding the significance of the name which actually means 'frolicsome'.

No records of figurehead designs exist for such a late period but the carvers created a three-quarter-length female figure with jewelled bangles on each wrist and, as an allusion to the 'frolicsome' description, the figurehead is painted with a domino mask of the type worn at masquerades.

National Museum of the Royal Navy.

While a significant number of warships that had completed their sea-service were taken to pieces in the royal dockyards, others were sold to commercial ship-breakers, notably to Henry Castle & Son. The firm was established in 1838 at Baltic Wharf, Millbank – very close to the present site of the Tate Gallery. Later it opened other ship-breaking yards on the Thames; Longs Wharf at Woolwich and Anchor & Hope Wharf at Charlton.

As can be seen in the photograph of their showrooms, they made garden furniture from serviceable wood but they also sold timber to the building trade and the residue was sold as logs. Just as in the dockyards, it was thought to be wrong to destroy the figureheads and these accumulated in the yards and were mounted in prominent places, occasionally being sold to customers.

In 1913, letters were published in *The Times* on how the nation's history would be better served if the figureheads from the Royal Navy's former ships were properly preserved. Philip Castle was moved to write that, if a place was found for such a scheme, he would offer any or all of the carvings in his care to the nation. Two of the figureheads featured in this book were transferred as a result of this offer – see Appendix I for HMS *Royal Albert* and Appendix III for HMS *Constance*.

Castles created their own small museum at Millbank that included figureheads and other decorative carvings but, sadly, this was destroyed in April 1941 during the London Blitz when the site suffered a direct hit by a high-explosive bomb.

Crown Copyright.

Crown Copyright.

By about 1900 the shape of a warship's bow and the material from which it was made had resulted in the figurehead becoming redundant. Despite this, there was still a need within the service for an emblem that represented the ship's name and with which the ship's company could relate. The ship's badge filled this gap, being informal in the early years of the twentieth century and then becoming formalised; initially with its shape identifying the size of the ship and more recently differentiating between seagoing ships, shore bases, etc.

Today each ship has a circular badge – with its device approved by the Naval Advisor on Heraldry – surrounded by a rope border and surmounted by a naval crown. The designs have naturally evolved over the years but the two examples shown here illustrate how the story told in the figurehead era for two of the ships represented in the Portsmouth collection of figureheads has continued into today's Royal Navy.

Appendices

APPENDIX I
Figureheads Formerly in the Collection

Hibernia	1804	Now in Malta
Royal Frederick	1841*	Decayed and destroyed
Royal Albert	1854	Decayed and destroyed
Royal Sovereign	1857	Decayed and destroyed

APPENDIX II
Other Carvings in the Collection

Poictiers	1809
Pigmy	1837
Queen Ann	1839
Victoria and Albert	1843
Victoria and Albert	1855
Alberta	1863
Albatross	1873

APPENDIX III
Other Figureheads in the Portsmouth Area

Queen Charlotte	1810	Whale Island
Vernon	1832	Gunwharf
Constance	1846	Whale Island
Supply	1854	Formerly at Royal Sailors Home Club
Marlborough	1855	Gunwharf
Ariadne	1859	Formerly HMS *Dryad*
Conway formerly *Nile*	1876	HMS *Nelson*
Martin	1890	Wardroom, HMS *Nelson*
Barfleur	1892	HMS *Nelson*
Victoria and Albert	1899	HMS *Nelson*
Seaflower	1873	Wardroom, HMS *Nelson*

Appendix 1

Figureheads Formerly in the Collection

HMS *Hibernia* – 1804-1902, *1st Rate, 110 guns*

Author's Collection.

The Ship

Built in Devonport Dockyard, she was the second ship to bear the name. In her early years she was involved in the blockade of Brest and later in an attack on the French batteries on their Mediterranean coast at Cassis. In 1814 she returned to England where she lay in reserve until 1845 when she was commissioned as the flagship to the Commander-in-Chief of the Mediterranean Fleet.

In 1855 she was docked in Devonport to be fitted out as the receiving ship at Malta and there she served in Dockyard Creek for almost fifty years before she was sold and broken up in Pieta Creek.

Design by Hellyer & Son dated March 1845. (TNA – ADM 87/15)

The Figurehead

No designs have been found for *Hibernia's* original figurehead that would probably have been made by the resident carvers at Devonport. The design for a replacement was submitted by Hellyer & Son of Portsmouth in March 1845, representing the Irish-Celtic god Dagda carrying a harp that he played to mark the change of the seasons. The carvers were allowed £47 for the work but were instructed to ensure that the figure on the harp did not extend beyond the line of the knee of the head and that the left arm of the main figure was to hold the harp within the line on the drawing.

When the ship was broken up the figurehead remained in Malta, at first by Dockyard Creek but in 1933 was relocated to the stone frigate, HMS *St Angelo*. There he remained until 1972 when, as part of the Royal Navy's withdrawal from Malta, he was shipped home to the National Museum of the Royal Navy at Portsmouth. He stood outside the Victory Gallery for over twenty years but then, as a result of approaches from the Maltese authorities, was returned to Malta where he arrived in July 1994 and is now in the Malta Maritime Museum.

HMS *Royal Frederick, Screw 1st Rate 121 guns, converted to an ironclad turret ship*

National Museum of the
Royal Navy.

The Ship

Named in honour of Frederick, Duke of York and second son of King George III, HMS *Royal Frederick* was ordered in September 1833 as a sailing 1st Rate ship but her build was suspended and she was re-ordered in June 1848 to be completed as a screw battleship. This decision was changed again in April 1859 when she was re-ordered as a screw two-decker and she was then renamed *Frederick William* in January 1860, on the day on which the Princess Royal married Prince Frederick William, later to become the German Emperor.

The Figurehead

As was appropriate for a ship named *Royal Frederick*, her figurehead was in the form of a bust of the Duke of York. The figurehead was designed by J.E. Hellyer of Portsmouth with an estimate of £46 for a standing figure or £35 for a bust, with extra for the trailboard carvings. The bust was approved in January 1835, £40 being allowed for the work.

With the reduction in the size of the ship, the figurehead was too large and was never fitted. It was, however, preserved in the dockyard and took its place at the entrance to the Dockyard Museum in the early years of the twentieth century (see page 17).

In what was no doubt a well-intentioned move to bring naval history to the young sailors of the day, the *Royal Frederick* figurehead and that of his companion *Royal Sovereign* were then moved to the parade ground of HMS *St Vincent*, the boys' training establishment in Gosport. They stood either side of the saluting dais, adding to the formality of a march past, but they could not withstand the effects of the weather and *Royal Frederick* was destroyed in 1957.

HMS *Royal Albert* – 1854-1884, *Screw 1st Rate, 121 guns, Battle Honour: Crimea 1854-55*

Richard Hunter Archive.

The Ship

Built at Woolwich Dockyard and launched there in May 1854, she had been ten years on the stocks and had been converted to steam prior to her launch. During her service career she was the flagship of the Black Sea Fleet in 1855 and the Channel Fleet in 1859 with a period in the Mediterranean Fleet in between. She was placed in reserve at Devonport in 1861 and was sold to Henry Castle & Sons, ship-breakers, in 1884.

Design by Hellyer & Son dated 1853.
(TNA – ADM 87/44)

The Figurehead

HMS *Royal Albert*'s figurehead was a three-quarter-length robed figure of Prince Albert, consort to Queen Victoria, holding a field marshal's baton in his left hand and wearing the insignia of the Spanish Order of the Golden Fleece.

It was carved by Hellyer & Son at their Blackwall workshop with an original estimate of £150, reduced to £100 after the royal arms intended for the trailboards had been declared 'not required' by the Surveyor of the Navy.

In 1913, after King George V had visited the Portsmouth Dockyard Museum, Mr Philip Castle of the ship-breaking company offered the figurehead to the museum, providing that it would be returned if ever the relic were to be disposed of. Measuring over 16ft tall, it was too large to fit in the museum and so was placed on a stone base near the Admiral Superintendent's office.

The elements must then have had their effect as, by the time the commands were required to report their holdings in 1957, there was no trace of this relic.

HMS *Royal Sovereign* – 1857-1885, *Screw 1st Rate 121 guns, converted to an ironclad turret ship*

National Museum of the
Royal Navy.

The Ship

One of the ships caught up in the transition of the fleet from sail to steam and the development of guns in turrets, HMS *Royal Sovereign* was ordered in June 1848 as a 1st Rate ship of 121 guns. She was re-ordered in June 1854 as a screw battleship and launched as such in April 1857 but was fitted for reserve service only. By August 1864 she had been cut down and converted to an ironclad ship with gun turrets.

The Figurehead

As was appropriate for a ship named *Royal Sovereign*, her figurehead was in the form of a crowned bust of Queen Victoria wearing the 'collar', sash and star of the Order of the Garter. The figurehead was designed by Hellyer & Son of Portsmouth and approved in July 1856.

When the ship was cut down in the 1860s the figurehead was replaced with a smaller carving in the form of a lion and Queen Victoria was preserved in the dockyard, taking her place at the entrance to the Dockyard Museum in the early years of the twentieth century (see page 17).

In what was no doubt a well-intentioned move to bring naval history to the young sailors of the day, the *Royal Sovereign* figurehead and that of her companion *Royal Frederick* were then moved to the parade ground of HMS *St Vincent*, the boys' training establishment in Gosport. They stood either side of the saluting dais, adding to the formality of a march past but they could not withstand the effects of the weather and *Royal Sovereign* was destroyed in 1946.

Appendix 11
Other Carvings in the Collection

HMS *Poictiers* – 1809-1857, *1st Rate, 110 guns*

National Museum of the
Royal Navy.

Named to commemorate the victory of Edward the Black Prince over the French at Poitiers in 1356, there was only one HMS *Poictiers* during the period of the 'Sailing Navy' – a 3rd Rate ship of seventy-four guns. Her figurehead stood over 9ft tall and was preserved, first at Chatham and later Sheerness, until it was found to be too rotten to save and was destroyed in the early years of this century.

This carving that is now on display with the Portsmouth figurehead collection was recorded in the 1911 Admiralty Catalogue as being at Chatham, not under the 'Figureheads' heading but that of 'Carvings', and is described as 'Carved Figure, Male (from "Poitiers")'. Since then, its movements can be traced;

first from Chatham to HMS *Ganges* at a date before 1962, and then to Portsmouth in 1976 when *Ganges* closed.

When described in *The Mariner's Mirror* in a 1913 article, it was noted that it was 'cut level at the back, presumably for attachment to a flat surface' and this feature – as well as its small size – would suggest that it was part of the stern carvings from the ship. It seems probable that, when the ship was taken to pieces in 1857 at Chatham, both the figurehead and this carving were taken into the Chatham collection and much later went their separate ways, the former to its eventual loss, the latter to its preservation in the Portsmouth collection.

HMS *Pigmy* – 1837-1879, *Wooden Paddle Packet, 227bm, 114ft*

Author's Collection.

Originally built by Humble & Hurry of Liverpool for the Post Office with the name *Sybil*, she was transferred to the Admiralty in April 1837 when the Admiralty assumed responsibility for the Packet Service. She was renamed *Pigmy*, was armed with a single 12-pounder carronade, and was based at Pembroke and Holyhead. She was used as a gunboat in the Baltic in 1854 and

then as a tender in Portsmouth, being broken up there in 1879.

Not qualifying for a figurehead, her bow decoration is in the form of a stylised Union Flag with a crown and the royal arms. It was listed in the first edition of the Portsmouth Dockyard Museum catalogue dated 1911 but not in the Admiralty Catalogue of the same date.

102

Queen Anne

National Museum of the
Royal Navy.

There has long been some doubt about the origin of the carving shown here. It is carved in the likeness of Queen Anne who reigned from 1702 to 1714 and whose statues may be found at Blenheim Palace and just outside St Paul's Cathedral in London. She is shown here wearing a crown and the 'collar' of the Order of the Garter.

Photographs of the carving first appeared in a 1938 report on the Chatham Dockyard collection when, for some unknown reason, she was listed as coming from HMS *Cleopatra*, a 6th Rate frigate of 1835. This identification was clearly doubted after she had been transferred to HMS *Ganges* as, in a 1949 report to the Commander-in-Chief on that collection, her photograph is marked 'Probably Queen Anne. Formerly Chatham Cat No 259'.

That 1911 Admiralty Catalogue entry – rather like the one for *Poictiers* above – is not under the heading 'Figureheads' but under one of 'Carvings' and is unnamed. Thus in 1911 Queen Anne was assessed not as a figurehead but as a supplementary carving and, as she has been cut flat at the back – like that from *Poictiers* – she too could well be from the stern carvings of a warship.

As the Royal Navy never had a ship with the name *Queen Anne*, it is impossible to say with any certainty from which ship she came. HMS *Queen*, a 1st Rate of 1839, would be a possibility; she had a three-quarter-length bust of Queen Victoria as her figurehead and this could have been complemented with a much smaller representation of Queen Anne in the stern carvings. We will probably never know.

HM YACHT *Victoria and Albert* – 1843-1854, *Royal yacht*, Renamed *Osborne 1854-1868, 225ft*

Author's Collection.

Built at Pembroke Dock and launched there in April 1843, she was the first of three royal yachts of this name built for Queen Victoria. A two-masted paddle steamer with a single funnel, she was powered by twin-cylinder engines manufactured by Maudslay & Sons.

After a successful maiden voyage that included Devon and Cornwall, France and Belgium, the Queen and Prince Albert used the yacht on regular cruises round the British coast – visiting major ports and making cross-Channel passages to meet the other crowned heads of state of Europe. When the next royal yacht was commissioned and named *Victoria and Albert*, this yacht was renamed *Osborne* after Osborne

House on the Isle of Wight, which the Queen had bought in 1845. She was taken to pieces at Portsmouth in 1868.

Victoria and Albert's bow decoration has the royal arms on the starboard side and Prince Albert's arms on the port side, held within a deeply carved scroll, the whole supported on carved roses, shamrocks and thistles. It was recorded in the 1911 catalogue of the Portsmouth Dockyard Museum as standing over the entrance of the Admiral Superintendent's office and can be seen there today a stone's throw away from the bow of HMS *Victory*.

HM YACHT *Victoria and Albert* – 1855-1904, *Royal yacht, 329ft*

National Museum of the
Royal Navy.

Right: Design by J.E. Hellyer dated
1854. (TNA – ADM 87/50)

As was her predecessor, she was built at Pembroke Dock and launched there in January 1855, the second royal yacht of this name built for Queen Victoria. Easily distinguishable from the original yacht, she was a three-masted paddle steamer and had two funnels. Her engines were made by Messrs Penn & Sons and were installed at Portsmouth Dockyard.

Known colloquially as *Victoria and Albert II*, she was used quite regularly by Queen Victoria and Prince Albert on home and cross-Channel visits but, after Albert's death in 1861, she was hardly used, except by members of the extended royal family. She was taken to pieces at Portsmouth in 1904.

Her bow decoration is similar to that of her predecessor, having the royal arms on the starboard side and Prince Albert's arms on the port side, again within a deeply carved scroll but in this case the whole being surmounted by a crown.

The carving was undertaken by Edward Hellyer of Blackwall who was allowed £45 for the double shield and an extra £16 for each trailboard. When the yacht was broken up, the carving was taken into the Portsmouth Dockyard collection and was recorded as being there in the 1911 Admiralty Catalogue.

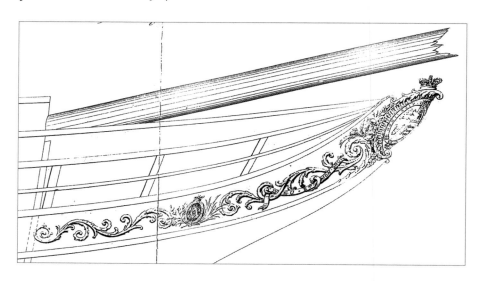

HM YACHT *Alberta* – 1863-1912, *Wooden paddle yacht, 391 tons, 160ft*

National Museum of the
Royal Navy.

Built at Pembroke Dock and launched there in October 1863, she was designed as the tender to the second Royal Yacht *Victoria and Albert*. Queen Victoria used *Alberta* extensively as she travelled between the mainland and her favourite residence, Osborne House, on the Isle of Wight.

When the Queen died at Osborne in 1901, it was natural that the first stage of her journey to Portsmouth, London and eventually her burial at St George's Chapel, Windsor, would be in *Alberta*. As one report put it: 'Then began the most beautiful naval ceremonial, the grandest and the saddest, that history records.'

While the two royal yachts named *Victoria and Albert* that pre-dated *Alberta* had bow decorations that contained both the royal arms and those of Prince Albert, the prince had died before *Alberta* was launched and so her bow decoration was carved in the simplified form of the royal arms in oval curved form surmounted by a crown and surrounded by gold scrolling. The decoration was carved by Frederick Dickerson of Devonport in 1863.

HMS *Albatross* – 1873-1889, *Composite screw sloop, 940 tons, 160ft*

National Museum of the
Royal Navy.

Built in Chatham Dockyard as one of six Fantome Class composite screw sloops, she is a good example of the transition from sail to steam with her three masts and single propeller, powered by an early compound engine made by Humphreys & Tennant. Her armament comprised two pivoted 7in and two pivoted 64-pounder muzzle-loading rifled guns firing through embrasures. She served both at home and on the China Station before being broken up at Chatham in 1889.

In keeping with the transitional nature of the ship, she was given a scroll rather than a figurehead, which suited her vertical bow, and yet it included a small albatross to represent the name of the ship.

When *Albatross* was broken up, her bow decoration was preserved in Chatham Dockyard and was still there when the collection was mustered in 1938. By 1949, when the Admiralty next assessed their figurehead holdings, the carving had joined the collection at HMS *Ganges* – the boys' training establishment at Shotley, Suffolk – one of a dozen figureheads and other relics that were displayed there in the 'Nelson Hall'. After the closure of HMS *Ganges*, the carving was transferred to the National Museum of the Royal Navy, arriving there in 1984.

Appendix III
Other Figureheads in the Portsmouth Area

HMS *Queen Charlotte* – 1810-1859, *1st Rate, 104 guns, 2,289bm, 190ft, Battle Honour: Algiers 1816*

Richard Hunter Archive.

The Ship
Built in Deptford Dockyard and launched there in May 1810, she was the second ship to be named after the queen consort of King George III, the first ship having accidentally caught fire and blown up off Leghorn in 1800.

In her first commission *Queen Charlotte* was involved in the blockading of Brest but she was paid off in Plymouth in August 1815 and became the guardship there and the flagship of Admiral Lord Exmouth. In 1816 she became Lord Exmouth's flagship of the Mediterranean Fleet and was joined by a Dutch squadron in the bombardment of Algiers – see HMS *Glasgow* on page 38 for more details.

She then returned to Portsmouth where she remained first as the guardship and later in Ordinary until in 1859 she was renamed HMS *Excellent* and became the gunnery ship and the start of a long association of that name with gunnery training. She was sold for breaking up in 1892.

The Figurehead
The figurehead is in the form of a bust of Queen Charlotte, wearing a state crown and a three-stranded necklace. When gunnery training moved ashore to Whale Island in 1891, the Queen came too and was mounted high up on the gabled end of an accommodation block near the entrance to the establishment. When these buildings were demolished in 2004, the figurehead was removed and resited on a plinth at the entrance to HMS *Excellent*.

HMS *Vernon* – 1832-1886, *4th Rate, 50 guns, 2,180bm, 176ft*

Author's Collection.

The Ship

Built at Woolwich Dockyard and launched there in May 1832, HMS *Vernon* was named after Admiral Edward Vernon, known chiefly for capturing a hoard of Spanish gold at Puerto Bello, Panama, in 1739. Vernon himself was also remembered in the navy as it was he who introduced the watering down of the rum ration. His nick-name in the fleet had been 'Old Grog', an allusion to the grogram material from which his clothes were made,

and so it was that diluted rum was always thereafter known as 'grog'.

After a period in the Experimental Squadron – designed to test the sailing abilities of various new types of vessels – *Vernon* saw service on the North America and West Indies Station, in the Mediterranean and finally in the East Indies. In 1870 she was used as a coaling jetty at Portland and then she became part of the Torpedo School for which her name is best known today. Joined by other decommissioned ships (see *Actaeon* on page 54 and *Warrior* on page 90) they made up the various components of the school, moving ashore to the old gunwharf in October 1923. She was sold for breaking up later that year.

Design by Hellyer & Son dated 1849.
(TNA – ADM 87/27)

The Figurehead

The figurehead that may now be seen close to the cafés in Gunwharf Quays is the second one fitted to the ship, carved in 1849 after Chatham Dockyard had reported that the original one was decayed. Hellyer & Son submitted a design showing the Vernon family arms with lion supporters and a crest consisting of a boar's head emerging from a baron's coronet. This was not approved and he was instructed to carve one 'in the likeness of the late Lord Vernon', as had originally been fitted to the ship. The resulting design was forwarded in November 1849, incorporating the Vernon arms in the trailboards, including the family motto *Vernon Semper Viret*.

The figurehead stood for many years in the grounds of the shore establishment HMS *Vernon*, and in May 2003, along with the figurehead of HMS *Marlborough*, was donated to the City Council as part of the Portsmouth Gateway Project to regenerate the harbour.

HMS *Constance* – 1846-1875, *4th Rate, 50 guns, 2,132bm, 180ft*

Richard Hunter Archive.

The Ship

Built at Pembroke Dock and launched there in March 1846, *Constance* was the third ship of what became a popular name for small ships, it being a quality that all would like to achieve.

She served on the Pacific Station for her first commission, assisting British traders in what would later become the west coast of Canada. In 1862 she was converted to steam propulsion at Devonport, an operation that involved her being cut in half and lengthened by 50ft to make room for the machinery, emerging as a steam-frigate with rather fewer guns. Thus provided with greater mobility, she saw service in the West Indies and around the east coast of Canada.

Returning to Devonport in 1868, she was decommissioned and remained there until she was sold for breaking up in 1875.

The Figurehead

With no figurehead carvers at Pembroke Dock-yard, the figureheads for the ships built there were carved in one of the other royal dockyards, Plymouth being preferred as the shipping costs were thus minimised. In June 1844 the Admiral Superintendent at Devonport forwarded a design by the resident carver there, Frederick Dickerson, with an estimate for £15; the sketch being unusual in that it was shown in colour.

There was then a period of some confusion. The figurehead was certainly carved by Dickerson but after a dispute about its size, the Surveyor sought an alternative from Portsmouth, receiving in August 1845 an estimate from Messrs Hellyer & Son of Cosham for £24. With the launch date approaching, the Hellyers were instructed to produce the figurehead without delay.

There has also been some debate on why the figurehead does not resemble that described by an admiral who had served in the ship as a young man. The suggestion is that, when the figurehead was transferred from the yard of Castles, the ship-breakers, she was confused with another carving. The jury is still out on this issue.

Design by Frederick Dickerson dated 1844. (TNA – ADM 87/14)

HMS *Supply* – 1854-1879, *Iron screw storeship, 638bm, 178ft*

National Museum of the
Royal Navy.

The Ship

Built by C.J. Mare of Blackwall on the Thames and purchased by the Admiralty while on the stocks, HMS *Supply* was launched in June 1854 and taken to the dockyard at Woolwich for fitting out.

Fitted with a G. & J. Rennie single-expansion trunk engine, she could steam at over 8 knots and provided stores to the fleet. She was broken up at Chatham in 1879.

The Figurehead

No references have been found in the Admiralty letters of the period to indicate whether *Supply*'s figurehead was carved before or after she was purchased in 1854. Carved as a female half figure with bunches of grapes held in both hands, her left breast is covered by a sash over her shoulder. Her hair is decorated with vine leaves and small bunches of grapes, suggesting the victualling stores that would have been included in the items that she provided to the fleet.

When the ship was broken up, the figurehead was taken into the Chatham collection where she remained until the early 1980s, initially in the Dockyard Museum and then in the vicinity of the Admiral's House. As part of the preparations for the closure of Chatham Dockyard, she found her way to Portsmouth and the custody of The Royal Sailors' Home in Queen Street, close to the Victory Gate of the dockyard.

By 2005 she was in a bad condition and was rescued for renovation by a figurehead historian and wood-carver from Gosport, Eric Walker. She has recently been acquired by the National Museum of the Royal Navy.

HMS *Marlborough* – 1855-1904, *Screw 1st Rate, 131 guns, 3,853bm, 245ft*

Author's Collection.

The Ship

Built in Portsmouth Dockyard, she was the fourth ship to bear the name, the first being named after the Duke of Marlborough in 1706, two years after his glorious victory over the French and Bavarians at the Battle of Blenheim. This 1855 ship was originally laid down in September 1850 as 120 gun 1st Rate but, as part of the transition from sail to steam, was re-ordered as a 131-gun screw battleship and launched as such in July 1855, one of the largest wooden warships ever built.

As the war with Russia was coming to an end, *Marlborough* was initially put in reserve but in 1858 she became the flagship of the Mediterranean Fleet, serving for six years before returning to Portsmouth as the receiving ship and later the engineers' training ship. In 1904 she was renamed *Vernon II* and became the accommodation ship of the Portsmouth Torpedo School (see also *Warrior* – 1860).

In 1923 the Torpedo School moved ashore into the old gunwharf and in 1924 *Marlborough* was sold for breaking up – but not before her figurehead was brought ashore with others that had been part of the afloat school.

The Figurehead

Marlborough's original figurehead was carved by J.E. Hellyer in his Blackwall workshop after some correspondence discussing whether it would be better to carve it at Portsmouth where the family also worked. The design shown below was approved at a cost of £50; a bust of the Duke of Marlborough with the trophies of war in the trailboards and a ribbon to celebrate the Battle of Blenheim.

Though undoubtedly the same subject, the surviving figurehead shows the Duke in armour and wearing the collar of the Order of the Garter so it would seem likely that, at some period of her fifty years of active naval service, she required a replacement and the present figurehead was carved. He stood for many years in the grounds of the shore establishment HMS *Vernon* and in May 2003 was donated to the City Council as part of the Portsmouth Gateway Project to regenerate the harbour. Since then he has stood looking out across the harbour from the residential part of the Gunwharf Quays development.

Design by J.E. Hellyer dated 1854. (TNA – ADM 87/50)

HMS *Ariadne* – 1859-1922, *Wooden screw frigate 26 guns, 3,214bm, 280ft*

National Museum of the
Royal Navy.

The Ship

Built in Deptford Dockyard, she was one of six ships known as 'Walker's Big Frigates' after their designer, Sir Baldwin Walker – Surveyor of the Navy. The design was intended to incorporate the lessons learned from the Crimean War and to match the steam frigates that were being built for the United States Navy. Armed with twenty-four 10in shell guns on the main deck and two 68-pounder guns on the upper deck, she had most of the features of a sailing frigate but with the addition of a Maudslay engine and single propeller.

In 1860 she was one of the ships that escorted the then Prince of Wales – later King Edward VII – on a memorable visit to Canada and the United States of America.

In 1876 she was attached to the hulk of HMS *Vernon* as officers' accommodation for those studying the new science of 'torpedo warfare and the application of electrics to gunnery'. In 1903 she was replaced in this role by HMS *Marlborough* (see page 110) and in 1905 she was renamed *Actaeon* and became the Torpedo School ship at Sheerness. There she remained until 1922 when she was sold for breaking up.

Design by Hellyer & Son dated 1858.
(TNA - ADM 87/68)

The Figurehead

In Greek mythology, Ariadne was the daughter of Minos, King of Crete. She helped Theseus slay the Minotaur but he then abandoned her on an island where, fortunately, she was found by Bacchus, the young god of wine. Bacchus and Ariadne were married and the crown that he gave her at their wedding he placed amongst the stars.

Ariadne's figurehead was carved by Hellyer & Son of Portsmouth in response to a Deptford Yard request for a figurehead to be provided; the carver's estimate for the work was £24.10.0. Note how the carver has alluded to the crown that Bacchus gave her in the trailboard carving.

There are significant differences between the 1858 design and the surviving figurehead – the style of her dress and the grapes and vine leaves in her hair – suggesting that the surviving figurehead is a replacement, carved at some stage of the ship's long period of service.

When HMS *Vernon* moved ashore the *Ariadne* figurehead was mounted outside the captain's house and there it remained until the land was sold for development into Gunwharf Quays. The carving has been restored and is now in Boathouse No.4 awaiting decisions on her future.

HMS *Conway* – 1876-1956, Formerly HMS *Nile 1839-1876, 2nd Rate, 92 guns, 2,589bm, 205ft,*
Battle Honour: Baltic 1854-55

Author's Collection.

The Ship

Built in Plymouth and launched there in 1839, HMS *Nile* was converted to steam propulsion there between 1852 and 1854. Having seen no sea-service before her conversion, she subsequently travelled widely, being awarded her Battle Honour 'Baltic 1854–55' and later becoming the flagship of the North American Squadron. After a period in reserve from 1864, she was adapted as a training ship and, in 1876, was loaned to the Mercantile Marine Service Association and her name changed to *Conway*.

Based at Liverpool, *Conway* saw generations of cadets passing through the training system but in May 1941, after several 'near misses' during the Liverpool Blitz, she was moved to a safer anchorage in the Menai Strait between Anglesey and the mainland. The cadets' training continued there.

In April 1953 when being towed back to Birkenhead for a refit, *Conway* ran aground close to the Menai Suspension Bridge and broke her back. The training of cadets went ashore to Plas Newydd on Anglesey.

The Figurehead

The design of *Nile*'s original figurehead was approved in 1831, carved probably by James Dickerson, the Devonport resident carver. The drawing on the right is the design for a replacement submitted by his son Frederick in 1851 while the ship was being converted to steam propulsion.

In June 1918 the SS *Bhamo* collided with the *Conway* and her figurehead was carried away. In 1937 the Conway Club of former cadets commissioned a replacement that was carved by Mr Carter Pearson and it was unveiled in September 1938.

Carved in a modern style, the figurehead shows Horatio Nelson in the uniform of a rear admiral, as that was his rank at the Battle of the Nile in 1798. He is wearing the star of the Order of the Bath and the gold medal presented after the Battle of St Vincent in 1797. The lower half of the carving is wrapped in a cleverly designed arrangement of bands carrying Nelson's signal at Trafalgar, 'England Expects That Every Man Will Do His Duty'. His left hand rests on a modern naval crown.

When the cadets' training went ashore on Anglesey the figurehead went too and remained there until training ceased in July 1974.

By chance, the name of the barracks at Portsmouth was at the same time being changed from HMS *Victory* to HMS *Nelson* and so it was decided that this would be an appropriate place for him. He stands a short distance inside the main entrance of the establishment and can be seen from the pavement of Queen Street.

Design by Frederick Dickerson dated 1851. (Private Collection)

HM BRIG *Martin* – 1890-1907, *Training Brig, 6 guns, 508bm, 100ft*

Crown Copyright.

The Ship

Built at Pembroke Dock and launched there in January 1890, she was one of seven training brigs attached to the various boys' training ships stationed round the coast in the last decade of the nineteenth century. *Martin* was attached to *St Vincent* – a 120-gun 1st Rate ship of the line that had become the training ship in Portsmouth Harbour in 1862 – taking the boys to sea and giving them early experience in working aloft and in general seamanship.

Instruction in handling sails was officially terminated in 1902 but continued in a half-hearted manner for a few more years and so *Martin*'s role came to an end. In 1907 she was decommissioned, stripped of her name and became a coal hulk – 'C 23' – serving the new steam navy.

See also HM Brig *Seaflower* (page 116).

The Figurehead

Martin's figurehead is a three-quarter-length female figure holding a gilded garland and with gilded tiara and floral trimmings to her dress. The carver would probably have included a martin in flight in the trailboards to identify the ship but this was not retained when the figurehead was removed from the ship.

This figurehead and that of *Seaflower* were mounted in 1906 in niches high on the front façade of the wardroom of HMS *Nelson* – immediately opposite the establishment's main gate. They can readily be seen from Queen Street.

HMS *Barfleur* – 1892-1910, *Battleship 10,500 tons, 360ft, Battle Honour: China 1900*

Author's Collection.

The Ship

Built in Chatham Dockyard and launched in 1892, she was the second ship to bear the name, commemorating the victory over the French fleet in 1692 off Cape Barfleur. One of two second class battleships designed for operation in the Far East with heavier guns than the Russian armoured cruisers on the Pacific Station and yet with a shallow draught to allow navigation of the Chinese rivers. Her sister ship was HMS *Centurion* whose figurehead is in the National Museum of the Royal Navy collection (see page 92).

After a period in the Fleet Reserve, she was commissioned in 1895 and served with the Mediterranean Fleet until 1898 when she sailed for the China Station. There she became flagship of the second-in-command, taking part in Allied operations in North China during the Boxer Rebellion and in the storming of Peking forts and Tientsin legations in 1900. She returned to Plymouth in 1901 for an extensive refit that included the removal of her figurehead. She was sold for breaking up in July 1910.

The Figurehead

Barfleur and *Centurion* were the last British battleships to have such embellishment on their bows, and the fact that *Barfleur*'s lion was removed in her 1902–04 refit showed that such decoration was considered unnecessary in the early twentieth-century navy.

The lion and royal arms were mounted on the roof of the Guard House at the main entrance of the Royal Naval Barracks, Portsmouth, and when this was rebuilt as an administration building, the carving was again incorporated. It can be seen from the pavement of Queen Street by looking over the main gate of HMS *Nelson*.

HM YACHT *Victoria and Albert* – 1899-1954, *Royal Yacht, 430ft*

Author's Collection.

The Ship

Built at Pembroke Dock and launched there in May 1899, she was the third royal yacht of this name to be built for Queen Victoria. Built of steel but clad with teak to give her a smarter appearance, she resembled her immediate predecessor with three masts and two funnels, but her larger engines and twin propellers made her four times as powerful.

Queen Victoria never set foot on her new yacht but King Edward VII used her extensively from 1901 to 1910 both at home and overseas. King George V made much less use of her during his reign from 1910 to 1936 – indeed she was laid up during the First World War. King George VI used her for his Coronation Review in 1937 and for one final tour to the West Country before the outbreak of the Second World War. *Victoria and Albert* was at first reduced to care and maintenance but was later moored beside Whale Island at Portsmouth where she served as overflow accommodation for the gunnery school, HMS *Excellent*.

Once decisions had been made for the replacement royal yacht *Britannia*, the fate of *Victoria and Albert* was sealed and in 1954 her fittings were removed and she was towed to Faslane in Scotland to be broken up.

The Bow Decoration

While similar in style to the decoration on the bows of the earlier royal yachts named *Victoria and Albert* (see pages 103 and 104), the arms of Prince Albert are not incorporated as he had died in 1861. The royal arms are enclosed in a richly carved scroll, decorated with the rose, shamrock and thistle.

It is today mounted before the mast at HMS *Nelson* and can be glimpsed through the railings from the pavement near the entrance to the establishment.

HM BRIG *Seaflower* – 1873-1908, *Training brig, 8 guns, 425bm, 100ft*

Crown Copyright.

The Ship

Built at Pembroke Dock and launched there in February 1873, she was another of the seven training brigs attached to the various boys' training ships stationed round the coast in the last decade of the nineteenth century. *Seaflower* was attached to *Boscawen* – formerly the 120-gun 1st Rate ship of the line *Trafalgar* (see page 62) – that in 1873 was renamed and became the training ship at Portland. *Seaflower*'s role was to take the boys to sea and give them early experience in working aloft and in general seamanship.

Instruction in handling sails was officially terminated in 1902 but continued in a half-hearted manner for a few more years and so *Seaflower*'s role came to an end. She was sold for breaking up in 1908.

See also HM Brig *Martin* (page 113).

The Figurehead

Seaflower's figurehead is a three-quarter-length female figure holding a red rose in her right hand and with gilded hairband and trimmings to her dress.

This figurehead and that of *Martin* were mounted in 1906 in niches high on the front facade of the wardroom of HMS *Nelson* – immediately opposite the establishment's main gate. They can readily be seen from Queen Street.

Glossary of Terms and Abbreviations

Battle Honours — Honours that are granted to HM Ships and Fleet Air Arm squadrons that have taken part in certain actions or campaigns. For more details see page 58.

Beakhead — In Tudor times the word describes the protruding part of the ship's bow. It was later used to describe the area forward of the forecastle and open to the sea.

Bowsprit — A large spar projecting over the bow of a ship.

Builders Measurement — (Shown in the headings as 'bm'.) A formula for calculating the tonnage of a ship based on her length and beam.

Busthead — A figurehead in the form of a bust, being the head, shoulders and chest but without arms.

Guard-ship — A warship stationed at a port to act as guard and usually the flagship of the port admiral.

Ironclad — The early name for warships built of iron or whose wooden hulls were protected by iron plates.

Mould-loft — A dockyard building with a large floor area where a ship's lines can be drawn to full size so that timbers can be cut or bent to shape.

Ordinary — When ships were not required for active service, they were laid up 'in Ordinary' with their masts, rigging, sails and guns stored ashore. They were fitted with temporary roofs to keep them dry.

Pitch Pine — A hard, heavy, resinous timber favoured by the navy for its figureheads.

Pounder (pdr) — The weight in pounds of the projectile fired by a gun.

Rate — The six divisions into which warships of the sailing navies were grouped according to the number of guns carried. For more details see page 76.

Receiving Ship — An old warship permanently moored in a naval port in which new recruits were accommodated until they were drafted to their sea-going ships.

Ropery Buildings — Buildings in which rope was spun for the rigging of ships and where the yarn was stored.

Ship of the Line — A warship in the days of the sailing navy that carried sufficient guns to serve in the line of battle.

Stem — The foremost timber forming the bow of the ship.

Stone Frigate — The generic term given to naval shore establishments to which personnel may be appointed.

Trailboards — The panelled area sweeping downwards and backwards from the figurehead onto which the carver's work could be continued. For more details see page 34.

Sources

Original Documents:

THE NATIONAL ARCHIVES OF ENGLAND & WALES

ADM 1/27038 and 269/33 – *Disposal of Figureheads from Sheerness and Chatham*
ADM 1/27846 – *Admiralty Muster of Figureheads 1957/58*
ADM 87 – *Surveyor of the Navy, In-Letters Relating to Ships (1806-1860)*
ADM 88 – *Surveyor of the Navy, Register of In-Letters Relating to Ships (1832-1860)*
ADM 91 – *General Letter Books of Navy Board and Admiralty Offices of the Comptroller and Surveyor of the Navy, Repair and Building of Ships – Out-Letters (1818-1860)*
ADM 106 – *Navy Board Records – In-Letters from Yards (1790-1832)*

MUSTERS BY NAVAL COMMANDS

D 9270/38 – *Figureheads in Dockyard, Royal Naval Barracks and Royal Naval Hospital, Chatham 1938*
MCD 13234 – *Figureheads at Chatham 31.12.48*
A Record of the Figureheads in HM Naval Establishments under Plymouth Command (Undated but *c.*1938)

Printed Works:

Admiralty, *Catalogue of Pictures, Presentation Plate, Figureheads, Models, Relics and Trophies at the Admiralty; on board H.M. Ships; and in the Naval Establishments at Home and Abroad* (Admiralty 1911)
Burns, Lt-Cdr K.V., *Plymouth's Ships of War* (National Maritime Museum, London, 1972)
Carr Laughton, L.G., *Old Ship Figure-Heads & Sterns* (Conway Maritime Press, 1991)
Colledge, J.J., *Ships of the Royal Navy* (Greenhill Books, London, 1987)
Cordingly, David, *Billy Ruffian, The Bellerophon and the Downfall of Napoleon* (Bloomsbury, London, 2003)
Dalton, Tony, *British Royal Yachts* (Halsgrove, Tiverton, 2002)
Fraser, Edward, *Bellerophon, The Bravest of the Brave* (Wells Gardner, Darton & Co. Ltd, London, 1909)
Frost, M.E.P, *Catalogue of Figureheads, Models, Pictures, Relics, Trophies, &c., H.M. Dockyard Portsmouth* (Gale & Polden Ltd, Portsmouth, 1911)
Grant, Michael and Hazel, John, *Who's Who in Classical Mythology* (Routledge, London, 1999)
Jackson, Lt P.H.O., *HMS Ganges Catalogue of the Collection in Nelson Hall and Museum* (Undated)

Lambert, Andrew, *Warrior: Restoring the World's First Ironclad* (Conway Maritime Press, London, 1987)
Lecky, Lt H.S., *The King's Ships* (Horace Muirhead, London, 1913)
Lyon, David, *The Sailing Navy List – 1688-1860* (Conway Maritime Press, London, 1993)
Lyon, David and Winfield, Rif, *The Sail & Steam Navy List – 1815-1889* (Chatham Publishing, London, 2004)
McGowan, Alan, *HMS Victory: Her Construction, Career and Restoration* (Chatham Publishing, London, 1999)
Manning, Capt T.D. and Walker, Cdr C.F., *British Warship Names* (Putnam, London, 1959)
Masefield, John, *The Conway – from her Foundation to the Present Day* (William Heinemann, London, 1933)
Moore, Sir Alan, Bt, *Sailing Ships of War 1800-1860* (Halton & Truscott Smith Ltd, London, 1926)
Norton, Peter, *Ships' Figureheads* (David & Charles, Newton Abbot, 1976)
Pack, Capt A.J., *The Origins of the Figurehead* (Headquarters Group, Royal Marines, Portsmouth, Undated)
Rankin, Stuart. *Shipbuilding in Rotherhithe – The Nelson Dockyard* (Rotherhithe Local History Paper No.2) (Dockside Studio 1996)
Sayer, Lt G.B., *HMS Vernon – a History* (The Wardroom Mess, HMS *Vernon*, Portsmouth, 1930)
Pengelly, C.A., *The First Bellerophon* (John Baker, London, 1966)
Stopford, T.P., *Admiralty Ships Badges – Original Patterns 1919-1994* (Stone Frigate, 1996)
Thomas, P.N., *British Figurehead and Ship Carvers* (Waine Research Publications, Wolverhampton, 1995)
Warlow, Lt-Cdr Ben, *Shore Establishments of the Royal Navy* (Maritime Books, Liskeard, 1992)
Warlow, Lt-Cdr Ben, *Battle Honours of the Royal Navy* (Maritime Books, Liskeard, 2004)
Winfield, Rif, *British Warships in the Age of Sail 1793-1817* (Chatham Publishing, London, 2005)
Winton, John, *The Naval Heritage of Portsmouth* (Ensign Publications, Southampton, 1994)

Indices

Visit our website and discover thousands of other History Press books.

www.thehistorypress.co.uk

The History Press